CW00392383

ELEMENTARY GREEK EXERCISES

Abbott & Mansfield
A PRIMER OF GREEK GRAMMAR

John Usher
AN OUTLINE OF GREEK ACCIDENCE

Hillard & Botting
ELEMENTARY GREEK EXERCISES
ELEMENTARY LATIN EXERCISES

North & Hillard
GREEK PROSE COMPOSITION
LATIN PROSE COMPOSITION
KEY TO GREEK PROSE COMPOSITION
KEY TO LATIN PROSE COMPOSITION

H. W. Auden
GREEK PHRASE BOOK

C. Meissner
LATIN PHRASE BOOK

ELEMENTARY
GREEK EXERCISES

AN INTRODUCTION TO

NORTH AND HILLARD'S

GREEK PROSE COMPOSITION

REV. A. E. HILLARD, D.D.
LATE HIGH MASTER OF ST. PAUL'S SCHOOL

AND

C. G. BOTTING, M.A.
LATE ASSISTANT MASTER AT ST. PAUL'S SCHOOL

DUCKWORTH

This impression 2003

Gerald Duckworth & Co. Ltd.
61 Frith Street, London W1D 3JL
Tel: 020 7434 4242
Fax: 020 7434 4420
inquiries@duckworth-publishers.co.uk
www.ducknet.co.uk

A catalogue record for this book is available
from the British Library

ISBN 0 7156 1524 6

Printed in Great Britain by
Antony Rowe Ltd, Eastbourne

PREFACE

THIS elementary book has arisen directly out of the needs of St. Paul's School, and it has been in use at St. Paul's School and at Colet Court Preparatory School for one term before publication. It was found a disadvantage to have no book definitely planned to lead up to North and Hillard's *Greek Prose*, which was in use from the Fourth Form upwards. The books tried were found to introduce unusual forms and much more vocabulary than was needed in the elementary stage. In these respects the present volume is made as simple as possible. The constructions introduced are only those which are required in order to introduce sufficient variety into the simple sentence. The vocabulary is confined to the commonest words, and no practice is given in rare types of declension. These are included in School Grammars for the sake of completeness, because the Grammar must be used in the course of translation, where a rare form may occur. But it is best to omit them altogether in the elementary stage of Greek writing.

In making the vocabulary small the authors aim at making it possible for pupils to learn it thoroughly. It is not unusual to find boys in the later stages of Greek Composition unable without continual reference to a dictionary to use even the commonest words.

For every three English-Greek exercises the authors have appended (pp. 113-140) one Greek-English exercise, carefully made to correspond to them in its vocabulary and its demand on the pupil's knowledge. It is meant to serve as a model for them; but the smaller number of these Greek-English exercises is due to the authors' opinion that an accurate knowledge of Greek Accidence is more quickly obtained by practice in turning sentences into Greek than by relying on translation from Greek.

As the exercises in this book are meant to accompany the learning of Greek Accidence, references are given at the head of each section to the corresponding sections in Abbott and Mansfield's *Primer of Greek Grammar* and in Rutherford's *First Greek Grammar*.

It is assumed that the pupil has practised writing the Greek alphabet and understands breathings. It is also assumed, that, as soon as he has learnt the forms, he is able, from his knowledge of Latin, to apply the following rules in making a Greek sentence :—

(1) An Adjective agrees in Gender, Number, and Case with the Noun which it qualifies.

(2) A Verb agrees with its Subject in Number and Person.

(3) The Subject of a Finite Verb is in the Nominative Case, and the Direct Object of a Transitive Verb is in the Accusative Case.

Apart from these, the Rules of Syntax are stated as they are required.

ELEMENTARY GREEK EXERCISES

Section I.

Grammar.—The Article : A.M. p. 24 : R. p. 4.
Feminine Nouns of 1st Declension :
A.M. p. 25 : R. p. 5.
Present Indicative of λύω : A.M. p. 72 : R. p. 66.

Rules.—(1) **Abstract nouns in Greek are preceded by the Article** (as in French) : thus

courage, ἡ ἀρετή.

(2) **A Possessive Genitive of a Noun is placed between the noun on which it depends and its Article** : thus

The wisdom of the Muse, ἡ τῆς μούσης σοφία.

But the Possessive Pronouns *my, our, your, his, their* may be translated by the Article simply until Ex. 139 is reached, where the Pronouns are dealt with.

He loosens his spear, λύει τὴν αἰχμήν.

Exercise 1.

1. I loosen the fetters.

2. In the sea.

3. The wisdom of the Muses.

4. In the country of the Muse.

5. They stop the battle.

6. You loosen the fetters.

7. The virtue of the Muse.

8. He stops the battle.

9. They loosen fetters.

10. The wisdom of the goddess.

Exercise 2.

1. We free the goddess.

2. You stop the battle.

3. Courage loosens the tongue.

4. The goddess of the country.

5. They stop the battles.

6. They free the Muses.

7. In the country of the goddess.

8. In the seas.

9. He loosens his fetters.

10. You free the goddesses.

Exercise 3.

1. The courage of the Muse.
2. The goddess of the sea.
3. The wisdom of the tongue.
4. We stop the battle in the country.
5. The goddess stops the battle.
6. He loosens the fetters of the goddess.
7. Wisdom stops battles.
8. You free the Muses.
9. They free the goddess of the country.
10. In the country of the Muses.

SECTION II.

Grammar.—Future Indicative of λύω : A.M. p. 72 : R. p. 66.

Exercise 4.

1. They will set free the army.
2. I pursue virtue and wisdom.
3. In the house of the goddess.
4. The goddess will prevent the victory.
5. We shall loosen our fetters.
6. They will pursue virtue.
7. The honour of the army.
8. They will prevent the goddess.
9. The victory of the Muses.
10. They will hunt in the land.

Exercise 5.

1. We shall stop the battles.
2. The goddesses will loosen the fetters.
3. He will pursue virtue and wisdom.
4. He will prevent the victory of the army.
5. In the houses of the Muses.
6. The Muse will loosen the fetters.
7. He pursues honour.
8. We shall prevent the victory.
9. He sets free the army of the country.
10 They will loosen their fetters in the house.

Exercise 6.

1. The honour of the Muse and the goddess.
2. They will free the army of the land.
3. The army pursues honour and virtue.
4. We shall prevent the victory of the goddess.
5. He will stop the battle.
6. The goddess will loosen the fetters.
7. The army will pursue victory.
8. In the house and in the sea.
9. You will prevent the victory of the army.
10. You will pursue honour.

SECTION III.

Grammar.—Masculine Nouns of 1st Declension:
A.M. p. 25 : R. p. 6.

Imperfect Indicative of λύω:
A.M. p. 72 : R. p. 66.

Exercise 7.

1. The steward was loosening his fetters.

2. We shall pursue the young man out of the land.

3. They were preventing the victory of the citizens.

4. We were setting free the judges.

5. You are stopping the battle.

6. I was pursuing the steward out of the house.

7. The army will pursue the citizens.

8. The victory of the citizens will free the army.

9. The citizens pursue honour and virtue.

10. The judge was loosing the steward.

Exercise 8.

1. The victory will loosen the tongues of the citizens.
2. The judge was pursuing the steward out of the house.
3. The citizens were stopping the battle.
4. I shall loose the steward of the land.
5. They pursue the judge out of the land.
6. Victory loosens the tongue of the young man.
7. They were hunting the citizens out of the houses.
8. The judges used to prevent the victory of the citizens.
9. The goddess was stopping the battle.
10. They were training the young men in wisdom.

Exercise 9.

1. The judges train the citizens in virtue.
2. They were hunting in the country.
3. You were pursuing virtue out of the land.
4. The Muses will train the young man in wisdom.
5. The courage of the citizen will stop the battle.
6. We were training the stewards in the houses.
7. The judges were loosening their fetters.
8. The army pursues the judges out of the land.
9. He is training the army in the country.
10. The citizens will pursue honour and wisdom.

SECTION IV.

Grammar.—Aorist Indicative of λύω : A.M. p. 72 : R. p. 68.

Exercise 10.

1. The sailors were pursuing the stewards.

2. He will train the soldiers in virtue.

3. The citizens pursued the young man to the gates.

4. The goddess prevented the victory of the soldiers.

5. They pursued the sailors into the sea.

6. They are training the sailor in wisdom.

7. The judges were pursuing the young man to the house.

8. He trained the soldiers in the country.

9. The soldiers pursued the sailor into the house.

10. The judge loosened his fetters in the house.

Exercise 11.

1. We hunted in the land of the judge.
2. The soldier loosened his fetters.
3. He pursued the soldier to the gate.
4. You hunted the young man out of the house.
5. The soldier will pursue wisdom in the country.
6. The judge stopped the battle of the citizens.
7. We trained the goddess in wisdom.
8. You pursued the steward out of the land.
9. They will pursue the sailor into the sea.
10. The victory loosened the tongues of the citizens.

Exercise 12.

1. The soldiers and sailors pursue honour.
2. The soldiers prevented the victory.
3. The goddess will train the sailor in virtue.
4. The citizens are pursuing the judge into the house.
5. The steward prevented the victory of the young men.
6. I pursued the judge to the gates of the house.
7. The soldier will free the judge of the land.
8. The sailors loosened their fetters in the house.
9. The victory of the sailors freed the army.
10. The sailors pursued the soldiers to the gates of the house.

SECTION V.

Grammar.—Masculine Nouns of 2nd Declension:
A.M. p. 26 : R. p. 7.
Perfect Indicative of λύω :
A.M. p. 72 : R. p. 68.

Rule.—**The instrument or means by which a thing is done is expressed in Greek by the Dative.**

We train young men by laws.
παιδεύομεν τοὺς νεανίας τοῖς νόμοις.

N.B.—A Vocative Case in Greek should always be preceded by the Interjection ὦ.

Exercise 13.

1. They pursued the men to the gate.

2. The general has trained the soldiers in war.

3. They pursued the sailor into the river.

4. The judges train the citizens in the law.

5. He has loosed the soldiers and sailors.

6. The men are pursuing the judges out of the land.

7. We have loosed the young men.

8. They will train the sailors in war.

9. The laws will prevent the judges.

10. The words of the general stopped the battle.

Exercise 14.

1. The general has not trained the citizens in war.
2. He will not prevent the battle.
3. The words of the man will stop the war.
4. The steward has loosened his fetters.
5. They pursued the general into the house.
6. We have trained the young man in virtue.
7. The victory of the general will stop the war.
8. The law of the citizens will prevent the battle.
9. He has not trained the judge in wisdom.
10. You have not loosened your fetters, young man.

Exercise 15.

1. By their valour the soldiers freed the citizens.
2. You will prevent the battle, general.
3. They stopped the war by their wisdom.
4. You have freed the sailor, O judge.
5. You have not trained the young men, citizens.
6. The war will train the soldiers and sailors.
7. You were pursuing the men into the river.
8. You prevented the battle by your words, O soldier.
9. The goddess has not trained the young man in virtue.
10. The general by his valour has freed the soldiers.

SECTION VI.

Grammar.—Neuter Nouns of 2nd Declension:
A.M. p. 26 : R. p. 7.
Pluperfect Indicative of λύω :
A.M. p. 72 : R. p. 68.

Rule.—**Neuter Plural subjects take a Singular Verb in Greek.**

The arms are in the house.
τὰ ὅπλα ἐστιν ἐν τῇ οἰκίᾳ.

Exercise 16.

1. The arms of the soldier are in the house.

2. The slave struck the head of the steward.

3. The horses were shaking their yokes.

4. He had loosed the slave of the judge.

5. You have struck the young man, general.

6. The soldiers are in the camp.

7. He will pursue the slave into the house.

8. We shook the horses' yokes.

9. The gifts of the judges are in the house.

10. We had brandished our arms in the battle.

Exercise 17.

1. The general of the army struck the judge.
2. The goddess had freed the slave by her deeds.
3. The slave had struck the horse of the general.
4. The sailors are in the river.
5. There are trees in the country.
6. The general's horse shook his yoke.
7. He had trained the citizens by his words.
8. The horses are shaking their yokes.
9. The soldiers freed the citizens by their arms.
10. The slave pursued the horse into the sea.

Exercise 18.

1. The gifts of the citizens are in the general's camp.
2. The horse of the slave is in the river.
3. The man struck the head of the judge.
4. He had prevented the battle by his words.
5. You have struck a man, O judge.
6. There are soldiers in the trees.
7. We shall brandish our arms in the war.
8. You had freed the sailors by your deeds.
9. There are rivers and trees in the land.
10. The weapons of the sailor are in the sea.

Section VII.

Grammar.—Feminine Nouns of 2nd Declension :
    A.M. p. 26 : R. p. 9.
    Adjectives of 1st and 2nd Declensions:
    A.M. p. 38 : R. pp. 33, 34.

Rule.—**Attributive Adjectives are placed between the Article and the Noun.**

    The wise man, ὁ σοφὸς ἄνθρωπος.

Exercise 19.

1. There are rivers and trees in the island.

2. He struck the head of the good slave.

3. The wise general freed the citizens.

4. He will train the clever young men in war.

5. The good judges prevented the war by their words.

6. You struck the head of the wise young man.

7. The friendly judges believed the words of the slave.

8. You pursued the man into the road, O sailor.

9. We trusted the friendly words of the general.

10. They trained the soldiers in an island.

Exercise 20.

1. They were not trusting the soldiers and sailors.
2. You stopped the war, O wise judge.
3. We shall prevent the battle by our words.
4. The good slave shook his head.
5. I trained the clever young man in the laws.
6. The friendly sailors are in the camp.
7. There are soldiers and sailors in the island.
8. They pursued the man from the house into the road.
9. We trust the words of the wise judge.
10. The laws are friendly to the good citizens.

Exercise 21.

1. The sailors pursued the man to the gates of the camp.
2. The gifts of the good judge are in the road.
3. The good slave loosed the horse.
4. The soldiers will not trust their general in the war.
5. They will pursue the citizens out of the island.
6. The good soldiers believed the judge.
7. The arms of the sailors are in the island.
8. They trusted the words of the friendly goddess.
9. I struck the head of the clever slave.
10. We shall pursue the sailors out of the island into the sea.

SECTION VIII.

Grammar.—Present and Imperfect Indicative of εἰμί :
A.M. p. 117 : R. p. 63.

Rules.—(1) Remember that **the complement of the verb** *to be*
is in the same case as the subject, just as in
Latin.

The citizens are free, οἱ πολῖται ἐλεύθεροί εἰσιν.

(2) **Do not use the Article with the complement.**

The young man was the general of the army.
ὁ νεανίας στρατηγὸς ἦν τῆς στρατιᾶς.

Exercise 22.

1. The courage of the soldiers was useful in the battle.

2. You are the general of the army.

3. The citizens are in the house of the young man.

4. The arms were the gift of the judge.

5. The general is often useful to the citizens.

6. The brother of the general is not a poet.

7. We were in the country of the Muse.

8. He often prevented a battle in the island.

9. They will pursue the poet out of the land.

10. The gifts of the sailors were in the sea.

Exercise 23.

1. There are useful trees in the island.
2. We shall pursue the poet to the gates.
3. The sea is useful to the sailors.
4. The soldiers were friendly to the citizens.
5. The horses were not useful in the war.
6. The rivers of the island are useful to the citizens.
7. The horse often shakes his head.
8. The citizens of the island are not free.
9. We were friendly to the judges.
10. The soldier will pursue his brother to the river.

Exercise 24.

1. The good judges were friendly to the general.
2. The clever poet trained his brother in wisdom.
3. Courage is useful in the war.
4. We were the stewards of the land.
5. The deeds of the general were useful in the battle.
6. The good judge will trust the laws.
7. The roads of the island were useful to the soldiers.
8. You were free citizens.
9. You will not stop the war, O poet.
10. The wise words of the general were useful in the war.

Section IX.

Grammar.—Future Indicative of εἰμί : A.M. p. 118 : R. p. 63.

N.B.—The Present Infinitive Active of Verbs in -ω is
formed by changing -ω to -ειν, *e.g.*

λύω, *I loose.*   λύειν, *to loose.*

Rule.—**Plural Nouns denoting whole classes take the
Article.**

Soldiers are brave (i.e. *all soldiers*).
οἱ στρατιῶται ἀνδρεῖοί εἰσιν.

Exercise 25.

1. The task will be difficult for the brave young man.

2. Slaves are not useful in war.

3. The head of the horse is beautiful.

4. The soldiers shook the beautiful trees.

5. We shall be the slaves of the young man.

6. The goddess often shakes the earth.

7. We trust the honourable words of the judge.

8. It is difficult to trust slaves.

9. There are useful trees in the island.

10. The base slave will be in the house.

Exercise 26.

1. You will be the general of the army.
2. The war was troublesome to the citizens.
3. The slaves will be brave in the battle.
4. He ordered the soldier to strike the horse.
5. It is difficult to shake the house.
6. They will be brave soldiers.
7. The words of the judge were honourable.
8. The brave sailor prevented the battle.
9. It is difficult to train young men.
10. Poets are not often brave.

Exercise 27.

1. It is disgraceful to strike slaves.
2. The citizens of the land will be free.
3. The wisdom of the general will be useful to the soldiers.
4. The tongue is useful to men.
5. You will not prevent the battle, O brave judge.
6. We shall not pursue the horses.
7. They struck the beautiful young man.
8. We shall not often be in the island.
9. We ordered the soldier to trust the judge.
10. They do not brandish their arms in the battle.

RECAPITULATORY EXERCISES

Exercise 28.

1. They will loose the beautiful goddess.

2. The wisdom of the poet will be useful.

3. The brave sailor stopped the battle.

4. They will hunt in the beautiful land.

5. He prevented the victory of the brave soldiers.

6. The honourable judges pursue virtue.

7. A brave sailor loosed the horse.

8. Good men trust the laws.

9. It is useful to train horses in war.

10. The judge ordered the man to loose the slave.

Exercise 29.

1. He pursued the base slave into the sea.
2. We shall trust the wise poets.
3. Arms are useful to a soldier in war.
4. It is difficult to train a base slave.
5. The victory of the brave general stopped the war.
6. He has not loosed the horse.
7. You will not be the general of the army, O brave poet.
8. The judge often used to strike the base slave.
9. The head of the horse is ugly.
10. They had brandished their beautiful arms in the battle.

Exercise 30.

1. You pursued the base young man out of the house.
2. By your wise words you have prevented the battle.
3. The brave slave loosed the horse of the judge.
4. They trusted the words of the wise goddess.
5. We shall be brave in the battle, general.
6. Good slaves are not often poets.
7. The task will not be difficult to a clever man.
8. The wise general was not in the island.
9. They will be the stewards of the land.
10. War is often useful.

PART II

SECTION I.

Grammar.—3rd Declension—Palatal Stems:
A.M. p. 31: R. p. 11.
Indicative Active of Palatal Verbs:
A.M. p. 79: R. p. 82.

Exercise 31.

1. The guards pursued the slave.

2. The herald fared badly in the battle.

3. We shall order the soldiers to train the slaves.

4. The guards were brandishing their arms.

5. The general will fare badly in the war.

6. We drew up the soldiers in the battle.

7. They have fared well in the house.

8. He ordered the guards to brandish their arms.

9. The slave struck the guard.

10. They trusted the words of the herald.

Exercise 32.

1. The generals will not fare well in the battle.
2. The guards of the island did not believe the herald.
3. They trained the sailors well.
4. They drew up the soldiers in the island.
5. The young men fared badly in the camp.
6. The citizens will not trust the heralds.
7. The heralds have fared badly in the road.
8. The clever general has drawn up the soldiers well.
9. Slaves often train horses badly.
10. The brave guards will pursue the citizens.

Exercise 33.

1. They transacted the affairs of the general badly.
2. He drew up the soldiers in the battle.
3. The slaves have fared well in the house.
4. The sailors pursued the guards.
5. He has not transacted the affairs of the citizens well.
6. We shall draw up the citizens in the road.
7. The heralds were in the island.
8. The judge believed the words of the herald.
9. He ordered the citizens to train the guards well.
10. The general will draw up the young men in battle.

Section II.

Grammar.—3rd Declension—Labial Stems: A.M. p. 33:

R. p. 12.

Indicative Active of Labial Verbs:

A.M. p. 79: R. p. 84.

Exercise 34.

1. He will send the soldiers into the camp.

2. He sent a herald to the island.

3. We have sent a herald to the camp.

4. They sent the poet to the house.

5. It will be useful to send a herald.

6. We shall send a herald to the island.

7. He has drawn up the soldiers in the road.

8. They have sent the man to the general.

9. We sent beautiful gifts to our brothers.

10. You have sent a slave to the judge.

Exercise 35.

1. The general sent a soldier to the house.
2. The sailor will pursue the herald.
3. You will send a present to the judge.
4. They send the sailors out of the camp.
5. The arms were useful to the guards.
6. It will be difficult to transact the affairs of the general well.
7. They have sent a present to the herald.
8. We sent a horse to the judge.
9. You sent the herald out of the camp.
10. The slaves transact the affairs of the young man well.

Exercise 36.

1. We sent the sailors to the sea.
2. The goddess fared badly in the battle.
3. They will order the general to send heralds.
4. They sent the herald to the gates.
5. The poets will fare badly in the camp.
6. They ordered the general to send his brother.
7. The deeds of the young men were disgraceful.
8. Poets are not useful in a battle.
9. The sailors transacted the affairs of the island.
10. They will send the brave soldiers to the war.

SECTION III.

Grammar.—3rd Declension—Dental Stems :
  A.M. pp. 31-33, § 46 : R. pp. 13-15.
  Indicative Active of Dental Verbs :
  A.M. p. 79 : R. p. 83.

Rule.—**Proper names commonly take the Article**

  Greece was then free.

  ἡ Ἑλλὰς τότε ἐλευθέρα ἦν.

Exercise 37.

1. The goddess preserved the country from war.

2. Old men transact affairs well.

3. We shall persuade the guards to save the country.

4. They pursued the lion into the sea.

5. The young men transacted the affairs of Greece.

6. He persuaded the young men to pursue virtue.

7. Young men do not believe old men.

8. You persuaded the slaves to loose your fetters.

9. We shall persuade the general to draw up the soldiers.

10. The free citizens will transact the affairs of Greece.

Exercise 38.

1. The soldiers by their courage preserved their country.
2. We persuade the general to stop the battle.
3. He will save the country from a terrible war.
4. You persuaded the judge to train the boys.
5. He will order the slave to pursue the lion.
6. The old men will preserve Greece by their wisdom.
7. They were persuading the soldiers to save Greece.
8. The good citizen will not believe the base slave.
9. The judge ordered the citizens to keep the laws.
10. Stewards then transacted the affairs of the house.

Exercise 39.

1. We ordered the young man to preserve his weapons.
2. The head of the lion will be terrible to the old man.
3. They ordered the slaves to preserve the beautiful trees.
4. Poets are not clever now.
5. The old men trusted the friendly heralds.
6. The deeds of the sailors were useful to Greece.
7. The brother of the judge has kept his weapons.
8. They persuaded the soldier to strike the horse.
9. It is difficult to persuade lions.
10. They will persuade the sailors to keep the laws.

SECTION IV.

Grammar.—3rd Declension : -Stems in λ, ρ, ν,
    A.M. p. 33 (§ 47), 34 (§ 48) : R. pp. 16-19.
    Numerals (Cardinal and Ordinal), 1-12 :
    A.M. pp. 53, 54 : R. pp. 54, 143, 144.

Rules for expressing Time.—

(1) **Duration of time is expressed by the Accusative.**
    He was in the island for three days.
    ἦν ἐν τῇ νήσῳ τρεῖς ἡμέρας.

(2) **Definite ' time when' is expressed by the Dative.**
    He transacted the affair on the third day.
    τὸ πρᾶγμα τῇ τρίτῃ ἡμέρᾳ ἔπραξεν.

(3) **Indefinite 'time when' and 'time within which' are expressed by the Genitive.**
    By night.   νυκτός.
    In (within) three days.   τριῶν ἡμερῶν.

Exercise 40.

1. He wrote a letter to the leader on the second day
2. He was in the house for three months.
3. In five days I shall persuade the judge.
4. The contest will be difficult for the young man.
5. We shall send a slave in six days.
6. For ten months they were in the island.
7. The citizens will trust the leader for three days.
8. In three days you will be the general of the army.
9. In seven days he will send a present to the leader.
10. By night the general writes letters.

Exercise 41.

1. He trains the young men by night.
2. He will persuade the general in four days.
3. For five months they transacted the affairs of the island.
4. The contest will be terrible for the Greeks.
5. He will write three letters in six days.
6. For eight days he was in the general's camp.
7. They will stop the war in nine days.
8. On the tenth day they will be in the island.
9. On the fourth day they pursued the herald out of the house.
10. They kept the letter for three months.

Exercise 42.

1. For eight months the leaders transacted the affairs of Greece.
2. He will be judge in the contests of Greece.
3. He often writes ten letters in three days.
4. They kept the letter of the judge for five days.
5. The arms of the young man were in the house for three months.
6. It is difficult to transact the affair well by night.
7. The general drew up the soldiers on the fourth day.
8. The citizens were free for ten months.
9. He will transact the affairs of his country for six months.
10. On the fifth day he sent a present to the judge.

PART III

SECTION I.

Grammar.—Middle of λύω—Pres. and Fut. Indic.:
  A.M. pp. 74, 76 : R. p. 70.
  Masculine Stems in ς: A.M. p. 34 : R. p. 20.
  Adjectives with Stems in ν and ς :
  A.M. p. 44 : R. pp. 47, 48.
Rule—**The Middle Voice has various meanings,
    the predominant idea being self-advantage :**
    e.g. λύομαι, *I loose for myself*, and so *I ransom.*
N.B.—An Adjective preceded by the Article may be used
  as a Substantive :
    The wise are not always good.
    οἱ σοφοὶ οὐκ ἀεὶ ἀγαθοί εἰσιν.

Exercise 43.

1. The citizens will ransom the soldiers.
2. We ransom the soldiers and sailors.
3. The kind general will ransom the men.
4. They will ransom the brother of Demosthenes.
5. You will not ransom Demosthenes, citizens.
6. The words of the herald were not true.
7. The nobles then transacted the affairs of Greece.
8. The kind judges stopped the contest.
9. We shall ransom the noble general.
10. There are arms in the house of the noble citizen.

Exercise 44.

1. The noble old man will ransom his horse.
2. The kind citizens will ransom the herald.
3. They have sent beautiful gifts to the noble general.
4. The nobles were not friendly to the slaves.
5. It is troublesome to transact the affairs of the leader.
6. The courage of Socrates was useful in the war.
7. The words of Demosthenes are true, citizens.
8. They pursued the nobles out of the land.
9. The citizens trusted Demosthenes in the battle.
10. They will ransom the old man in three months.

Exercise 45.

1. We do not ransom slaves in war.
2. The Greeks will persuade the nobles to save their country.
3. They wrote a letter to the kind leader.
4. He persuaded the young man to pursue the lion by night.
5. We shall send a letter to the noble leader.
6. The slaves trusted the noble judges.
7. You wrote a letter to the kind old men.
8. In four months they will ransom the nobles.
9. The slaves will trust the noble leader.
10. Terrible will be the contest, citizens.

Section II.

Grammar.—Middle of λύω—Imperfect and Aorist Indicative:

A.M. pp. 74, 76 : R. pp. 70, 72.

Neuter Stems in ς : A.M. p. 34 : R. p. 20.

Exercise 46.

1. In three years they will send a herald to Greece.

2. They used to ransom the soldiers in the wars.

3. You did not ransom the clever poet, citizens.

4. In summer the nobles pursue lions.

5. The kind leaders ransomed the poet.

6. We shall ransom the brother of the young man.

7. The judge was not friendly to Demosthenes.

8. The citizens ransomed the noble general.

9. He is not friendly to the race of poets.

10. True is the word of the wise poet.

Exercise 47.

1. In summer they will cease from war.
2. They will pursue the noble leaders for three days.
3. The soldiers ceased from the battle.
4. They will not ransom the clever poet.
5. We sent three letters to Demosthenes.
6. The kind leaders will stop the war in six days.
7. In the third year the Greeks sent a herald.
8. We were ceasing from the battle on the fifth day.
9. The race of slaves is not friendly to the poets.
10. Terrible will be the contest for the nobles.

Exercise 48.

1. They are ransoming the noble young man.
2. We believed the true words of the slave.
3. They will cease from war on the fourth day.
4. In summer lions are not friendly to men.
5. They transact the affairs of the old man in summer.
6. We ransomed the good slaves and brave guards.
7. It is useful to pursue lions in summer.
8. They were ceasing from the terrible battle.
9. He will ransom his noble brother.
10. We persuaded Socrates to write a letter.

SECTION III.

Grammar.—Middle of λύω—Perfect and Pluperfect Indicative : A.M. p. 74 : R. p. 72.

Stems in ι : A.M. p. 29 : R. p. 21.

Exercise 49.

1. The noble generals transacted the affairs of the city.

2. The kindly judge has ransomed his brother.

3. We had ransomed the wise poet.

4. They will not cease from the terrible war.

5. They sent a herald to the city.

6. He had ransomed the brother of the young man.

7. The noble leader has ransomed the steward.

8. The citizens have ransomed the general.

9. The power of the city was terrible.

10. The leaders had ransomed their slaves.

Exercise 50.

1. The battle had ceased on the fifth day.
2. There were beautiful trees in the island then.
3. The generals have ransomed the brave slave.
4. The judge ransomed his steward.
5. The nobles ceased from the contest.
6. It is disgraceful to transact the affairs of the city badly.
7. We have ransomed our slaves.
8. He has ransomed his brother by beautiful gifts.
9. The brave soldiers saved the city by their courage.
10. We sent the old man to the gates of the city.

Exercise 51.

1. The island is beautiful with trees in summer.
2. You have ransomed your brother.
3. They had ceased from the battle.
4. The arms of the kind general will be useful to the old man.
5. We trusted the laws of the city.
6. The country of the old man was free.
7. The wise poet transacts the affairs of the city well.
8. In three months they will ransom the guards of the city.
9. The nobles have ceased from the war.
10. The races of Greece were not friendly to the herald.

SECTION IV.

Grammar.—Passive of λύω—Aorist Indicative :

A.M. p. 74 : R. p. 74.

N.B.—The forms of the Present, Imperfect, Perfect and Pluperfect of the Middle Voice are also used with the Passive meaning.

Noun Stems in υ : A.M. p. 29 : R. pp. 21, 22.

Adjectival Stems in υ : A.M. p. 39 : R. p. 38.

Rule.—**The Agent by whom an action is performed is expressed by** ὑπό **with the Genitive Case.**

Exercise 52.

1. The words of the poet were pleasing to the citizens.
2. The slave was freed by the noble general.
3. The battle was prevented by the goddess.
4. The brave slaves are being set free.
5. The sailors pursued the man to the broad river.
6. There are beautiful fishes in the river.
7. We were freed by the noble old man.
8. The words of the judge were short.
9. The slaves have been freed by Socrates.
10. You were freed by the brave soldiers, Demosthenes.

Exercise 53.

1. In summer it is pleasant to cease from our tasks.
2. There are beautiful fishes in the seas of Greece.
3. Greece was freed by the brave leaders.
4. The battle had been prevented by Demosthenes.
5. The words of the noble old man were pleasing to the citizen.
6. It was pleasant to transact the affairs of the kind judge.
7. They sent three letters to Demosthenes on the tenth day.
8. The citizens trusted the pleasant words of the herald.
9. The slaves were being freed by the generals.
10. It is pleasant to write a letter to Socrates.

Exercise 54.

1. The rivers of the land are not broad.
2. The battle was prevented by the wise old man.
3. Sweet to the poet are the words of the Muse.
4. The contest is being stopped by the judge.
5. In three months they will ransom the poet's brother.
6. The kind citizens persuaded the general to stop the battle.
7. The war was stopped by the friendly goddess.
8. Greece was freed by the valour of the citizens.
9. There are fishes in the broad rivers.
10. The gifts of the soldiers were pleasing to the noble general.

SECTION V.

Grammar.—Passive of λυω—Future Indicative :
A.M. p. 74 : R. p. 74.
Noun Stems in Diphthongs : A.M. p. 30 ᵢ
R. p. 23.

Exercise 55.

1. The battle will be prevented by the general.

2. The gifts of the king were pleasing to the citizens.

3. The old man transacts the affairs of the king.

4. You will be set free in five days.

5. The general drew up the cavalry.

6. Their fetters were loosened on the tenth day.

7. The king's brother will be set free.

8. The cities will be freed in three months.

9. Pleasing words are not always true.

10. It is difficult to believe the king of the Persians.

Exercise 56.

1. The city will be freed by the sailors in five days.
2. The cavalry saved the citizens by their arms.
3. Horses are useful to Persians in battle.
4. We shall be freed by the bravery of the slaves.
5. The Greeks sent a herald to the king.
6. The sailors did not trust the cavalry.
7. The roads of the island are broad.
8. He will be prevented by the kind judge.
9. We used to ransom our kings in war.
10. They pursued the king to the gates of the city.

Exercise 57.

1. He has not sent a letter to the king.
2. The country of the Persians will be free in five years.
3. We were prevented by the heralds of the king.
4. The soldiers pursued the cavalry out of the land.
5. There are broad roads and beautiful trees in the island.
6. It is pleasant to transact the affairs of the Persians.
7. We pursued the king's herald out of the city.
8. Greece will not be freed by cavalry.
9. The battle was prevented by the king.
10. Kings do not always pursue virtue.

PART IV

SECTION I.

Grammar.—Present and Imperfect Indicative, Active and
Passive, of Verbs in -*aω* : A.M. pp. 84, 85:
R. pp. 76, 77.

Exercise 58.

1. The boys honoured the wise poet.

2. The soldiers honour their general.

3. We honoured the laws of our country.

4. The Greeks used to honour the gods by contests.

5. The children of Socrates were in the road.

6. He is honoured by the general of the Greeks.

7. The rhetorician trained the boys for three months.

8. He wrote a letter to the orator on the tenth day.

9. They persuaded the boys to pursue virtue.

10. It is difficult for an orator to transact the affairs of the
city.

Exercise 59.

1. We are honoured by the old man.
2. They believed the sweet words of the orator.
3. Poets are not always friendly to orators.
4. In summer the boys and young men pursue lions.
5. True words are pleasing to the gods.
6. You are honoured by the citizens of Greece.
7. The children of the general were in the broad road.
8. It is pleasant to train boys in wisdom and virtue.
9. The judge is honoured by the king.
10. The leader of the cavalry was honoured by the citizens.

Exercise 60.

1. Brave men are always honoured by poets and orators.
2. The city honours the king of the Persians.
3. We honour the brave guards of the city.
4. The king sent gifts to the clever boys.
5. The gods were honoured by the old men.
6. The nobles are honoured by the wise citizens.
7. The orators saved Greece by their true words.
8. The laws of the city are honoured by the poet.
9. He is honoured by the free citizens.
10. We honour the brave leaders of the cavalry.

SECTION II.

Grammar.—Special 3rd Declension Liquid Stems:
A.M. p. 33 : R. p. 19.
Present and Imperfect Indicative, Active and
Passive, of Verbs in -εω : A.M. pp. 86, 87 :
R. pp. 76, 77.

Exercise 61.

1. The King of the Persians treated the slaves badly.

2. The children believed the true words of their father.

3. Mothers love their children.

4. The city is loved by the free citizens

5. We love wars and battles.

6. We treat our generals badly.

7. The children will ransom their father in five days.

8. Socrates is loved by the wise citizens.

9. I used to love and honour the judge.

10. The boys loved their father and mother

Exercise 62.

1. The fathers trained their children in virtue.
2. We love and honour the race of poets.
3. Old men are loved by wise young men.
4. The leaders are loved by their soldiers.
5. It is difficult for a father to strike his child.
6. In three years they will ransom the boy's father.
7. The gift of the fish was pleasing to the king.
8. The boys believed the words of their wise mother.
9. We love and honour our fathers and mothers·
10. He is loved by the king's slaves.

Exercise 63.

1. We treated the slaves of Demosthenes badly.
2. The city will cease from the terrible war in eight months
3. The boys' father prevented the contest by his words.
4. They persuaded the mother to trust the boy.
5. The citizens treated the king's herald badly.
6. They sent the boy to his father's house.
7. Greece is loved by good citizens.
8. We were treated well by the king of the Persians.
9. The rhetorician is honoured and loved by the boys.
10. Wars are not pleasing to mothers.

Section III.

Grammar.—The Noun ἀνήρ : A.M. p. 33 : R. p. 25.

Present and Imperfect Indicative, Active and
Passive, of Verbs in -οω :
A.M. pp. 88, 89 : R. pp. 76, 77.

Exercise 64.

1. The men showed courage in the battle.

2. The boy shows his father's valour.

3. The judge was showing his wisdom.

4. You are not showing valour in the war.

5. Greece is being enslaved by the Persians.

6. The valour of a man is shown in battle.

7. He used to enslave free citizens.

8. Greece will be free in four years.

9. Courage was shown by the soldiers in the war.

10. The guards of the gates were useful to the citizens.

Exercise 65.

1. The city was being enslaved by the wicked general.
2. He enslaves the free citizens of Greece.
3. He sent the men to the camp of the Persians.
4. We do not enslave Greeks in war.
5. The king of the Persians was showing courage.
6. You are not showing your wisdom, citizens.
7. We love and honour the gifts of the Muse.
8. The children were well treated by their mothers.
9. The wise father is loved by his children.
10. The brave boy showed courage in the contest.

Exercise 66.

1. The boys were well treated by the rhetorician.
2. The sailors were showing courage in the battle.
3. The stewards of the house used to treat the slaves badly.
4. A good man does not enslave his brothers.
5. He persuaded the father to believe his children.
6. We Greeks do not enslave free citizens.
7. The words of the orators were pleasing to the young men.
8. The courage of the soldier is shown by deeds.
9. The poet was loved by his brother.
10. There are beautiful trees in the broad roads.

SECTION IV.

Grammar.—Irregular Nouns: A.M. p. 36: R. pp. 26, 27, 29.
The Adjective μέλας: A.M. p. 42: R. p. 39.
Future, Aorist, and Perfect Indicative Active and
Passive of Contracted Verbs:
A.M. pp. 85, 87, 89: R. pp. 80, 81.

N.B.—Be careful to note that Verbs in -αω, εω, -οω
are only contracted in the Present and Imperfect
Tenses: the other tenses are declined like the corresponding tenses of λύω.

Exercise 67.

1. The women will show courage in battle.
2. There are black ships in the river.
3. The general has treated the soldiers badly.
4. The sailors loosed the black ship.
5. The citizens honoured the king's wife.
6. We will show valour in the contest.
7. The women believed the pleasing words of their
   husbands.
8. A good boy will honour his father.
9. We love the free citizens of Greece.
10. The brave soldier honours his country.

Exercise 68.

1. The Greeks will not honour the king of the Persians.
2. The courage of the cavalry was shown in the battle.
3. The children of the Persian honoured courage and wisdom.
4. He has always honoured the noble general.
5. The children of Socrates did not always honour their mother.
6. In summer there are black ships in the river.
7. The words of Demosthenes were not pleasing to the citizens.
8. In three years you will enslave Greece.
9. The black ship was loosed by the sailor.
10. The good slave has done the task well.

Exercise 69.

1. By night and day the rhetorician is training boys.
2. Greece will honour the brave men by contests.
3. The task was done by the boys and slaves.
4. Greece does not now honour the gods by contests.
5. In six months the Persians will enslave the free city.
6. The wife of the king wrote a letter on the sixth night.
7. He will show his father's courage in the battle.
8. A brave woman is not always honoured by her husband.
9. The king is enslaving the free cities of Greece.
10. They persuaded the sailors to loose the black ships.

PART V.

SECTION I.

Grammar.—Infinitives of λύω, Active, Middle, and Passive.
A. M. pp. 73, 75, 77 : R. pp. 67, 69, 71, 73, 75.

N.B.—The Aorist Infinitive may refer to present time no
less than the Present Infinitive. The difference
between the two will be explained later on, but the
sentences in the following exercises are such that
the pupil will not be wrong in any case whether he
uses the Aorist or the Present Infinitive in Greek
as the equivalent of the English Present Infinitive.

E.g. He ordered the slave to loose the horse.

$$\acute{\epsilon}\kappa\acute{\epsilon}\lambda\epsilon\upsilon\sigma\epsilon\ \tau\grave{o}\nu\ \delta o\hat{\upsilon}\lambda o\nu \begin{Bmatrix} \lambda\acute{\upsilon}\epsilon\iota\nu \\ \lambda\hat{\upsilon}\sigma a\iota \end{Bmatrix} \tau\grave{o}\nu\ \emph{ἵππον}.$$

Exercise 70.

1. It will be easy to loose the black ship.
2. It was difficult to write the letter by night.
3. The Greeks formerly showed valour in war.
4. He persuaded the man to ransom his slave.
5. He will persuade the nobles to send heralds.
6. It will be difficult to cease from the war.
7. It is disgraceful to have trusted the words of the slave.
8. They persuaded the old man to ransom his children.
9. We ordered the soldiers to cease from the battle.
10. It will not be difficult to persuade Demosthenes.

Exercise 71.

1. In summer it is pleasant to have ceased from labours.
2. He easily persuaded Demosthenes to draw up the soldiers.
3. It will not be difficult to prevent the battle.
4. It is not difficult for a boy to believe his mother's words.
5. We shall persuade the judge to stop the contest.
6. It is easy to brandish arms in battle.
7. It will be honourable to have freed our country.
8. He ordered the steward to manage the affairs of his house.
9. We were formerly honoured by our slaves.
10. The wise king was formerly loved by the citizens.

Exercise 72.

1. The words of Socrates will not be pleasing to the young man.
2. The power of the king was terrible.
3. The nobles were loosed by the slaves.
4. It will be difficult to cease from war.
5. Courage was often shown by slaves.
6. We are not always honoured by our children.
7. He will persuade the king to ransom the leader.
8. The general of the Persians drew up the cavalry well.
9. He ordered the young man to ransom his father.
10. It is always difficult to write letters by night.

SECTION II.

Grammar.—Present, Future, and Aorist Participles Active of
λύω : A.M. pp. 40, 41 : R. pp. 41, 43, 73.

Rules.—(1) **A Relative Clause in English may often be
translated in Greek by the Participle preceded by the Article.**

Those who save their country are honoured.
οἱ τὴν πατρίδα σῴζοντες τιμῶνται.

(2) **The Present Participle describes an action as
going on at the same time as the action of
the main verb, the Aorist Participle as having
occurred before it.**

While pursuing the lion he displayed courage.
θηρεύων τὸν λέοντα ἐδήλωσε τὴν ἀρετήν.
Having written the letter he sent it.
γράψας τὴν ἐπιστολὴν ἔπεμψεν.

Exercise 73.

1. Those who prevent battles show their wisdom.
2. We honour those who believe their fathers.
3. The general trusts all his soldiers.
4. The orator, having persuaded the citizens, ceased.
5. The Persians enslaved all the cities.
6. Having loosed the slaves, they sent a letter to the king.
7. We honour those who save their country.
8. All men trust the wise judge.
9. In three days all the cities will be free.
10. We love those who often write letters.

Exercise 74.

1. All the women were set free by the general.
2. He who persuades the citizens is honoured by all.
3. Those who often write letters are not always loved.
4. Having sent a soldier, he persuaded the king.
5. Those who trust their leaders prosper in battles.
6. Having ordered the slave to loose the horse, he wrote a letter.
7. We do not always love the prosperous.
8. Having prevented the battle he sent his soldiers into the camp.
9. The bad are not often prosperous.
10. Bad boys do not believe their fathers and mothers.

Exercise 75.

1. Those who brandish their arms are not always brave.
2. It is disgraceful to strike a brother.
3. He who saves his country is loved by all.
4. We trust those who manage the affairs of Greece.
5. It is easy for the prosperous to keep the laws.
6. He persuaded the father to send his boy to Greece.
7. For three years the Greeks prospered in the war.
8. He who trusts the king of the Persians is enslaving his country.
9. Having persuaded the citizens, Demosthenes will cease from his speech.
10. He who is prosperous is not always well treated by the citizens.

SECTION III.

Grammar.—Active Perfect Participle and the Middle Participles of λύω : A.M. pp. 40, 75: R. pp. 46, 71, 73.

Exercise 76.

1. We honour those who fight for their country.

2. Those who have freed their slaves are loved by all.

3. We honour those who ransomed the soldiers.

4. It is easy for the prosperous to cease from work.

5. He will persuade the king to fight in ten days.

6. We sent the slave to the Persians' camp.

7. Those who manage the affairs of Greece are honoured by all.

8. He who saves his country is loved by all the citizens.

9. The words of orators are pleasing to women.

10. The old man trusted all his slaves.

Exercise 77.

1. Those who have shown courage are honoured by all.
2. The woman's children were trained by rhetoricians.
3. The young men saved the city by their courage.
4. The useful slave managed all the old man's affairs.
5. Those who cease from work are not wise.
6. Those who ransom the nobles will not be serving their country.
7. He who fights for Greece will not love the Persians.
8. Women then managed the affairs of their houses.
9. The old man honoured those who had ransomed his children.
10. Those who drew up the cavalry saved the city.

Exercise 78.

1. Those who obey their fathers will prosper.
2. The king trusts those who fight for their country.
3. We honour those who have benefited the city.
4. The words of the mother were not pleasing to the king.
5. Those who obey their general serve their country.
6. We shall not enslave those who fight for Greece.
7. Having ceased from his speech he drew up the cavalry.
8. It is difficult to obey a bad king.
9. We all love those who have served their country.
10. You all show courage in battle.

Section IV.

Grammar.—Passive Participles of λύω:
> A.M. p. 40 : R. p. 42.
> The Adjective χαρίεις : A.M. p. 40 : R. p. 40.

Exercise 79.

1. Those who had been set free were in the harbour.

2. There are graceful women in the island.

3. Having been set free by the king, they honoured the Persians.

4. He does not honour those who fight badly.

5. Those who were set free by the general were useful in the battle.

6. There were soldiers and sailors in the harbour.

7. We love those who prosper in war.

8. Those who are being sent into Greece are honoured by all.

9. We do not trust those who were set free by the leaders.

10. The graceful woman loved her children.

Exercise 80.

1. Those who obey the guards will be set free.
2. The graceful women did not trust the orator's words.
3. The citizens did not honour those who were set free.
4. Those who are fighting will cease from the contest in three months.
5. He who fights for his country is honoured by all the Greeks.
6. Those who have been set free are in the city.
7. The bad orators persuaded the citizens by their pleasing words.
8. Those who ransomed the poet were loved by the citizens.
9. The king of the Persians has not prospered in the war.
10. We have sent a herald to those who are fighting.

Exercise 81.

1. Those who are ordered to fight do not always obey.
2. We honour those who stopped the battle.
3. Those who wrote the letter did not trust the herald.
4. Men showed courage in the contests of Greece.
5. The citizens, having been set free, will benefit their country.
6. The kind general has benefited his country.
7. A brave young man shows courage in contests.
8. There were sailors and soldiers in the ships.
9. The nobles managed the affairs well for three years.
10. Those who obey the king of the Persians will not be useful citizens.

PART VI

SECTION I.

Grammar.—Active Imperatives of λύω : A.M. p. 72 :

R. pp. 66, 69.

The Adjective πολύς : A.M. p. 42 : R. p. 50.

Rule.—**Commands are expressed in the Imperative.**[1]

Train your children.

παιδεύετε τοὺς παῖδας.

Loose the horses, slave.

λῦσον τοὺς ἵππους, ὦ δοῦλε.

Exercise 82.

1. Order the soldiers to cease from the battle.
2. Brandish your arms, guards.
3. There are many ships in the harbours of Greece.
4. Set free those who have benefited the city.
5. Much bravery was always shown by the sailors.
6. Stop the contest, judge.
7. Save your country by your courage, soldiers.
8. Order your sons to obey the rhetorician.
9. Many of the Greeks fared badly in the battle.
10. Order all the citizens to obey the general.

---

[1] There is a difference between the uses of the Present and of the Aorist, but this difference will be explained later. In the sentences of the following exercises the pupil may use either the Present or the Aorist.

Exercise 83.

1. Many tasks are easy for a young man.
2. The herald ordered all the cities to obey the king.
3. Trust those who fight well for their country.
4. The king of the Persians enslaved many cities.
5. Draw up the cavalry, general.
6. Believe the words of the king, citizen.
7. Send a herald to the leader of the army.
8. Pursue lions in summer.
9. For many years the cities obeyed the king.
10. Terrible is the power of the many.

Exercise 84.

1. There were formerly many races in Greece.
2. Believe the true words of Demosthenes, citizens.
3. Let boys believe their fathers and mothers.
4. Persuade the nobles to keep the laws. ·
5. The mother was always kind to her children.
6. For many years all the cities were free.
7. The many do not always trust the nobles.
8. Persuade the citizens to ransom the generals.
9. Let him write a letter to his father.
10. Persuade the judges to set Socrates free.

Section II.

Grammar.—Middle and Passive Imperatives of λύω:
A.M. pp. 75, 76 : R. pp. 70, 72, 74.

The Adjective μέγας : A.M. p. 42 : R. p. 50.

Exercise 85.

1. Ransom the leaders, citizens.

2. Great is the power of the nobles.

3. Let the brave slaves be set free.

4. Obey the true words of Socrates.

5. Persuade Socrates to train the boys in wisdom.

6. Let them ransom their brave generals.

7. The boys will not pursue the great lion.

8. Many women manage the affairs of their houses well.

9. They pursued the lion to the great gates.

10. There are many rivers and large trees in the island.

Exercise 86.

1. Order the boys to send many gifts to their fathers.
2. Many of the slaves showed courage in the war.
3. Let the citizens be set free by the nobles.
4. Let them ransom those who saved their country.
5. It will be difficult to pursue the great lion.
6. Obey your father, young man.
7. Fight well, soldiers, and save the city.
8. Let the arms be brandished in the camp.
9. Great deeds are not always difficult.
10. Let them believe the true words of Demosthenes.

Exercise 87.

1. Let women manage the affairs of the house.
2. The many will not save the city.
3. It is always difficult to persuade the king.
4. Let men manage the affairs of the state.
5. He persuaded the old man to write the letter.
6. Great was the power of the Greeks.
7. Obey the wise judge, citizen.
8. We shall save our country by our arms.
9. Let the letter be written by night.
10. Ransom your son, old man.

SECTION III.

Grammar.—Active Subjunctive of λύω : A.M. p. 72:

R. pp. 67, 69.

Rules.—(1) **Exhortations** (which are equivalent to commands in the 1st person) **are expressed by the Subjunctive.**

> *Let us fight well.*
>
> εὖ μαχώμεθα.

(2) **Prohibitions** are of two kinds :—

  (a) **General,** *in which the prohibition is a* **general rule** : *expressed by* μή *with the* **Present Imperative.**

> *Do not believe bad men.*
>
> μὴ πίστευε τοῖς κακοῖς.

  (b) **Particular** : *in which a* **particular instance** *is forbidden : expressed by the* **Aorist Subjunctive.**

> *Do not do this.*
>
> μὴ ποιήσῃς τοῦτο.

N.B.—**The Negative used with the Imperative and Subjunctive Moods is** μή, **not** οὐ.

Exercise 88.

1. Do not order the boy to write the letter.
2. Let us prevent the battle by our words.
3. Do not send gifts to bad boys.
4. Let us draw up the soldiers in the city.
5. Do not persuade boys to fight.
6. Do not trust the pleasing words of the king.

7. Let us pursue virtue and wisdom.
8. The teeth of the lion were sharp.
9. Do not loose the black ship, sailor.
10. Let us always trust our fathers and mothers.

Exercise 89.

1. Do not send the young man to the city.
2. Let us write a letter to the king of the Persians.
3. Do not draw up the cavalry now.
4. Do not brandish your arms in battle.
5. Let us trust the kind words of the king.
6. Do not trust the nobles.
7. The sharp teeth of the lion will be terrible to the slaves.
8. Do not write letters by night.
9. There are many kinds of lions in the island.
10. Do not draw up the cavalry in the road.

Exercise 90.

1. Do not stop the contest, judge.
2. Obey your leaders, and do not trust the king.
3. Do not pursue the old man out of the city.
4. All the citizens of Greece will then be free.
5. For six months the leader was honoured by the citizens.
6. We love those who accomplish many tasks.
7. They were honoured by those who had saved their country.
8. Do not trust the guards of the city.
9. Let us not send a herald to the camp.
10. The lion's teeth were sharp and terrible.

Section IV.

Grammar.—Middle and Passive Subjunctives of λύω :

A.M. pp. 75, 77 : R. pp. 71, 73, 75.

Exercise 91.

1. Let us not obey the king of the Persians.

2. Do not cease from the war now, citizens.

3. Do not ransom the wicked king.

4. Do not fight on behalf of bad men.

5. Let us not be prevented by the words of the poet.

6. The general drew up the cavalry in front of the walls.

7. Do not trust those who are transacting the affairs of the city.

8. We shall not enslave those who obey their generals.

9. Let us fight well on behalf of our country.

10. Let us ransom the noble king.

Exercise 92.

1. Do not be persuaded by pleasing words.
2. Do not send the boy to Greece.
3. Let us not cease from the contest.
4. Do not believe all men.
5. Let us not be persuaded by orators.
6. All the ships were not in the harbours.
7. There are many kinds of poets and orators.
8. Let us obey the wise old men.
9. Send a herald in three days.
10. Do not strike bad slaves.

Exercise 93.

1. We honour the words of the wise poet.
2. Let us not fight in front of the city.
3. Do not always trust clever young men.
4. The cavalry were drawn up in front of the walls.
5. Let us preserve our great walls.
6. The teeth of the lion were large and sharp.
7. There are many kinds of fish in the rivers.
8. You do not honour those who fight for the king.
9. Those who accomplish many tasks are not always loved.
10. Do not send heralds to all the cities.

SECTION V.

Grammar.—Active Optatives of λύω: A.M. p. 73:

R. pp. 67, 69.

Rule.—**Wishes for the Future** are always to be expressed by the **Optative** [Present or Aorist tense] with or without the particles εἴθε or εἰ γάρ. **Negative** μή.

> *May you not accomplish the task !*
>
> μὴ πραξείας τὸ ἔργον.
>
> *May they not fare ill in the battle.*
>
> εἴθε μὴ κακῶς πράττοιεν ἐν τῇ μάχῃ.

Exercise 94.

1. May the Greeks prosper in the war !

2. Oh that the goddess may prevent the battle !

3. May you not fare badly in the battle !

4. Oh that we may not transact the affairs badly !

5. Do not trust the race of poets.

6. Let us not send the ships into the harbour.

7. Oh that you may persuade the king to fight !

8. Do not order the slaves to fight.

9. Let us not harm those who have benefited their country.

10. Oh that he may not draw up the cavalry in front of the walls !

Exercise 95.

1. May you save your country, young man!
2. Those who harm the city are not loved by the gods.
3. Oh that we may save the walls of our city!
4. Let us draw up the cavalry in the broad road.
5. They will easily accomplish the task in twelve days.
6. Oh that they may not harm the ships!
7. The words of the orator will be short.
8. The gods honour those who obey.
9. Women do not always trust their husbands.
10. The soldiers will be drawn up in front of the walls.

Exercise 96.

1. There are beautiful and graceful women in the island.
2. Oh that the general may not stop the contest!
3. Do not harm those who saved their country.
4. Let us always trust the gods.
5. Let us not always obey the nobles.
6. They sent the fish to the great king.
7. The power of the city was shown in the war.
8. The gods are not kindly to those who injure their country.
9. You are all honoured by the king.
10. The power of the city is shown by the deeds of the citizens.

SECTION VI.

Grammar.—Middle and Passive Optatives of λύω:
A.M. pp. 75, 77 : R. pp. 71, 73, 75.

Rule.—**A phrase which qualifies or describes a Noun is usually put between the Noun and its Article,** *like a Genitive depending on it.*

> *The fish in the river.*
> οἱ ἐν τῷ ποταμῷ ἰχθύες.

N.B.—(1) πᾶς *used in the Singular without the Article means* '*every,*' *with the Article* '*the whole.*'

> *Every city.* *The whole of the city.*
> πᾶσα πολις. ἡ πᾶσα πόλις, *or* πᾶσα ἡ πολις.

(2) *Two adjectives agreeing with one noun are coupled by* καὶ *in Greek.*

> *Many beautiful trees.*
> πολλὰ καὶ καλὰ δένδρα.

Exercise 97.

1. May the slaves not be set free by the king !
2. Oh that you may obey the words of your father !
3. Let us preserve the trees in the island.
4. Let every city send soldiers.
5. May you not be prevented by the leader of the Persians !
6. Oh that the king may fight in ten days!
7. The soldiers in the camp did not love their general.
8. Oh that we may not be stopped by the judge !
9. Let us not ransom the whole army.
10. Oh that every citizen may fight well for his country !

Exercise 98.

1. Oh that the orator would cease from his speech!
2. May he not be prevented by the old man's words!
3. May you all prosper in Greece!
4. There are many beautiful trees in the island.
5. On the third day he drew up the cavalry in front of the city.
6. Let us write a letter to the children of Socrates.
7. The many are often harmed by the nobles.
8. In three years the gods will save the whole of Greece.
9. May they not be prevented by the words of the wicked!
10. It is easy to harm those who administer the affairs of the state.

Exercise 99.

1. The roads in the island are large and broad.
2. We do not love those who stopped the contest.
3. The words of the mother were short and sharp.
4. The whole island was beautiful with trees.
5. We honour those who obey the gods of their country.
6. Let us send many brave soldiers to Greece.
7. Oh that they may obey those who administer the affairs of the city!
8. Do not write many letters in summer.
9. Do not order the guards to harm Socrates.
10. There are many beautiful harbours in Greece.

PART VII

SECTION I.

Grammar.—Active Voice (in full) of Contracted Verbs
in -αω : A.M. p. 84 : R. pp. 76, 78, 80.
Regular Comparison of Adjectives in -ος :
A.M. p. 50 : R. p. 51.

Rule.—**Where two things are directly compared with one
another by means of a Comparative Adjective,
use the Genitive of Comparison in Greek.**

The Greeks are braver than the Persians.

οἱ ῞Ελληνες ἀνδρειότεροί εἰσι τῶν Περσῶν.

Exercise 100.

1. Men are not always wiser than women.
2. Do not honour those who obey the king.
3. The war will be very terrible for the citizens.
4. He ordered the boy to honour his mother.
5. May they not honour the king of the Persians !
6. It will be more difficult to persuade the boy.
7. Oh that the Greeks may conquer the Persians !
8. The Greeks were more free than the Persians.
9. Orators are not always wiser than generals.
10. The Greeks conquered their conquerors.

Exercise 101.

1. The ships in the harbour are beautiful.
2. Do not honour the conquerors.
3. Men are braver than women.
4. We love those who honour virtue.
5. May I always honour those who saved their country !
6. The many have always honoured the nobles.
7. A bad boy will not honour his mother.
8. The father of the judge was very wise.
9. Honour your father and obey the laws.
10. May you conquer the Persians, general !

Exercise 102.

1. The whole city will honour the bravest leader.
2. Socrates was the wisest of all men.
3. Good citizens will always honour Demosthenes.
4. Of all men the Greeks were the most free.
5. Let him honour his country and his king.
6. The Greeks will easily conquer the army of the king.
7. It will be most difficult to conquer the Persians.
8. Those who conquer in war are honoured by all.
9. Let us not always honour the conquerors.
10. May you always honour old men !

SECTION II.

Grammar.—Middle and Passive Voices (in full) of Contracted

Verbs in -*αω*: A.M. p. 85 : R. pp. 77, 79, 81.

Exercise 103.

1. May the king be always honoured !

2. Let us not be conquered by the Persians.

3. The Greeks will be conquered in three days.

4. Those who are honoured by the king are very rich.

5. Let the Greeks be honoured by all. .

6. It is pleasant to be honoured by the many.

7. There are many rich men in Greece.

8. The wisest men in the city will honour Demosthenes.

9. May we not be honoured by the bad !

10. The Persians were richer than the Greeks.

Exercise 104

1. It will not be difficult to defeat the cavalry.
2. May the gods be honoured by all!
3. It is easy to be honoured by the many.
4. The teeth of the lions were large and sharp.
5. Those who are honoured by the citizens will not harm the city.
6. Do not write letters to the rich.
7. Oh that Demosthenes may not be defeated in the battle!
8. Do not defeat those who fight for their country.
9. The rhetorician was honoured by all the boys.
10. Do not trust those who are honoured by the king.

Exercise 105.

1. The nobles in the island were very rich.
2. Do not believe the words of the conquered.
3. The soldiers were braver than the sailors.
4. Do not pursue the Persians to their ships.
5. The cavalry were easily defeated by the king.
6. The words of the orator will be honoured by all.
7. Socrates was wiser than Demosthenes.
8. Those who are defeated are not honoured by their conquerors.
9. We were honoured by the bravest citizens.
10. Every island will then be free.

SECTION III.

Grammar.—Active, Middle, and Passive Voices (in full)
of Contracted Verbs in -εω : A.M. pp. 86, 87 :
R. pp. 76-81.

Exercise 106.

1. Let us always love our benefactors.

2. Do not treat your slaves badly.

3. Those who benefit their country are honoured.

4. We shall carry on the war in the winter.

5. Do not believe those who are loved by the king.

6. The city is loved by the citizens.

7. Every city was carrying on the war with much courage.

8. May we always honour the bravest soldiers !

9. We do not trust those who are carrying on the war.

10. Let us carry on the war against the king with much
    courage.

Exercise 107.

1. The whole city was benefited by those who administered the affairs.
2. The gods will not harm those who benefit their country.
3. Do not love those who harm the city.
4. May they not carry on the war for many years!
5. Oh that you may benefit your king and country!
6. Let us persuade the citizens to carry on the war with much courage.
7. May he always love his father and mother.
8. It is disgraceful to harm our benefactors.
9. Do not trust those who persuaded the king to fight.
10. The conquerors were richer than the conquered.

Exercise 108.

1. It was disgraceful to fight against our benefactors.
2. May we not treat badly those who saved the country!
3. Let us ransom those who have benefited the city.
4. Do not love those who honour war.
5. The conquered are wiser than the conquerors.
6. All the cities of Greece were free for many years.
7. Let us carry on the war for six months.
8. Greece has not been benefited by the orators.
9. The sons of the free citizens were trained in wisdom.
10. Do not carry on the war in the winter, citizens.

SECTION IV.

Grammar.—Active, Middle, and Passive Voices (in full)
of Contracted Verbs in -οω :
A.M. p. 89 : R. pp. 76-81.
Regular Comparison of Adjectives in -ας
and -ης : A.M. p. 50 : R. p. 51.

Exercise 109.

1. All the ships will be safer in the harbour in winter.

2. Do not enslave the noblest citizens.

3. It is disgraceful to enslave those who fight for their
   country.

4. Most true were the words of the conquerors.

5. Those who enslaved Greece are not honoured now.

6. May you always show courage in battle !

7. It will be safest to trust the king's words.

8. Let us not be enslaved by the Persians.

9. Those who show courage are loved by boys.

10. Let us not send presents to those who enslaved the city.

Exercise 110.

1. The conquerors will be more free than those who are enslaved.
2. May we always show courage in war, citizens.
3. It will be safer to carry on the war in spring.
4. Those who fight are nobler than those who are enslaved.
5. Those who honour the gods are the noblest of all.
6. Oh that Greece may not be enslaved by the king!
7. Do not enslave the brave leader of the cavalry.
8. Much wisdom will be shown by the judge.
9. The whole city was enslaved by the great king.
10. Those who fight before the walls will be safest.

Exercise 111.

1. The men in the ships were safer than those fighting in the city.
2. Much courage was shown by all the women.
3. In spring and summer the island will be beautiful with trees.
4. In three months we shall carry on the war with much courage.
5. Oh that the many may not be enslaved by the nobles!
6. The sons of free men are wiser than slaves.
7. The richest citizens do not always benefit their city.
8. Wisdom is very useful in war.
9. Show courage in the battle, oh bravest of all men.
10. It will be most difficult to carry on the war in the spring.

PART VIII

SECTION I.

Grammar.—Conjugation of Palatal Verbs:
A.M. pp. 76-81 : R. pp. 82, 164.
Regular Comparison of Adjectives in *-ων* :
A.M. p. 51 : R. p. 52.
Rules of Reduplication : A.M. pp. 91, 92 :
R. p. 163.

N.B.—*Aorists ending in -σα, such as* ἔλυσα, *are called* **First** (*or*
Weak) Aorists. *Some Verbs with Consonant Stems*[1] *have
another type of Aorist, ending in -ον, called the* **Second**
(*or* **Strong) Aorist.**
E.g. φεύγω, *I fly.*   ἔφυγον, *I fled.*

**The Second Aorist of the Active Voice has the same terminations
as the Imperfect in the Indicative Mood, and as the Present
in other Moods.**

Exercise 112.

1. The work was easily accomplished in five days.
2. All those who were defeated fled to the camp.
3. The most temperate men have sacrificed to the gods.
4. The Greeks will not flee out of the country.
5. The difficult task has been accomplished by the sailors.
6. Those who were enslaved by the king have fled in the night.
7. You did not flee to the walls, soldiers.
8. The priests have sacrificed to the gods of Greece.
9. Do not flee from the army of the Persians.
10. We shall not honour those who fled out of the city.

---

[1] These are not confined to any particular class of Consonant Stems,
and the pupil can only learn them as he learns the Vocabulary.

Exercise 113.

1. He has sought his benefactor in every city.
2. The soldiers have guarded the walls of the city well.
3. Everything was accomplished in six months by the priest.
4. We shall flee into the country of the Persians by night.
5. On the third day the words of the king were more kindly.
6. The more temperate men had sacrificed to the gods.
7. Having been defeated, we fled to the camp.
8. You will not flee from the gods, young man.
9. Socrates was the most temperate of all the Greeks.
10. The city was guarded by sailors and soldiers.

Exercise 114.

1. Those who avoided Socrates did not love virtue.
2. We seek the most temperate men in the city.
3. Let us flee from those who are guarding the city.
4. Those who sacrificed to the gods have prospered in the battle.
5. Those who harm their country will not flee from the gods.
6. Having been honoured with gifts they trusted the words of the herald.
7. The walls were guarded by the bravest citizens.
8. It will be safer for the women to fly out of the city.
9. The task has been accomplished by the leader of the cavalry.
10. The conquerors were more temperate than the conquered.

SECTION II.

Grammar.—Conjugation of Dental Verbs:
  A.M. pp. 76-81 : R. pp. 83, 164.
  Comparative and Superlative of μέγας:
  A.M. p. 51 : R. p. 52.
  Declension of μείζων : A.M. p. 44 : R. p. 49.
  Rules of Augment : A.M. p. 90 : R. p. 157.

N.B.—(1) *The endings -νται in the Perfect Indicative Passive, and
  -ντο in the Pluperfect Indicative Passive, are incom-
  patible with Consonantal Stems : in these cases the peri-
  phrasis with εἰμί is employed.*

  E.g.   They have been persuaded, πεπεισμένοι εἰσίν.
      They had been persuaded, πεπεισμένοι ἦσαν.

(2) Note that the Aorist Indicative Passive of Dental Verbs
  (*i.e.* with Present in -δω, -θω, and sometimes -ζω) usually
  ends in -σθην.

  E.g. πείθω, I persuade.   *ἐπείσθην, I was persuaded.*
  *An exception is σώζω, which has Aorist Indicative Passive
  ἐσώθην.*

Exercise 115.

1. The Greeks were not deceived by the pleasant words of
   the king.
2. The greatest cities were enslaved by the conquerors.
3. Those who tell lies do not honour the gods.
4. We were willing to honour the greatest poet.
5. Greece was saved by the courage of those who carried
   on the war.
6. Those who were trained by the orator were not willing
   to guard the city.
7. We were perplexed when fighting against the cavalry.
8. They have been persuaded by the graceful woman.
9. We deceived the old man by pleasant words.
10. The greater poets were not willing to honour the king.

Exercise 116.

1. Let us not be deceived by the herald of the Persians.
2. All the ships fled into the harbours of Greece.
3. Being perplexed, he told lies and would not obey.
4. The greatest ships are not always the safest.
5. The most temperate men would not honour the king.
6. The cavalry were drawn up in front of the walls.
7. The richest men sent the greatest gifts.
8. Demosthenes, the greatest orator, was often perplexed.
9. The power of the Greeks was then greater.
10. The women will not be deceived by the words of the orator.

Exercise 117.

1. Oh that the Greeks may not be persuaded to harm Socrates !
2. It will be disgraceful to carry on the war on behalf of the king.
3. The general of the Greeks was perplexed.
4. Let us not be persuaded to enslave free citizens.
5. The Greeks were not willing to fight in winter.
6. Those who do everything for their country are loved by all.
7. They have been deceived by the pleasant words of the herald.
8. The bravest men will be drawn up in front of the gates.
9. Being perplexed we would not trust the leader.
10. The women were saved by the brave slaves.

SECTION III.

Grammar.—Conjugation of Labial Verbs:
  A.M. pp. 76-81 : R. pp. 84, 164.

  Comparison of πολύς: A.M. p. 51 : R. p. 53.

Exercise 118.

1. The poets asked for very many gifts.

2. Gifts were sent to the boy by his mother.

3. The soldiers, having left their ranks, asked for arms,

4. Do not leave the old man in the city.

5. Those who were left in the land asked for many things.

6. They left very many ships in the harbour.

7. Most gifts were sent by those who had prospered in the war.

8. The Persians have conquered and the gods have forsaken the city.

9. Being perplexed, we left all the women in the ships.

10. May you not be sent out of the city to the king !

Exercise 119.

1. Those who were sent did not ask for arms.
2. We deceived those who were left in the city with pleasant words.
3. Very many cities were carrying on the war with much courage.
4. It will be safest to leave all the women in the city.
5. The soldier, having been saved by his general, fled to the harbour.
6. Oh that the soldiers may not leave their ranks!
7. The cavalry were sent to the camp by their leader.
8. Let us not ask for many gifts.
9. It will be safer to leave the children in the house.
10. Being perplexed they fled to Demosthenes.

Exercise 120.

1. Most true were the words of those who were sent by the king.
2. There are very many kinds of fishes in the river.
3. The task was easily accomplished by those left in the city.
4. Those who ask for everything are not loved by most people.
5. Very many gifts were sent to the prosperous.
6. Persuaded by Demosthenes, the citizens will carry on the war with great courage.
7. Those who were saved were perplexed, and asked for arms.
8. The greatest poets are not always honoured by their fellow-citizens.
9. We fled by night out of the harbour into the town.
10. Everything will be accomplished in three days by those left in the city.

SECTION IV.

Grammar.—Liquid Verbs: A. M. pp. 76-81: R. pp. 85, 161, 164.

Comparison of καλός :   A.M. p. 51 : R. p. 53.

Exercise 121.

1. The Athenians fitted out ten ships.

2. The ships were equipped in twelve days.

3. The soldiers will fly to the mountains.

4. The most temperate men did not advise the Athenians to fit out ships.

5. The richest men had many houses.

6. They announced everything to the king of the Persians.

7. We had most beautiful horses and very many houses.

8. They equipped very many ships when fighting against the Persians.

9. We shall have very many ships and very brave soldiers.

10. The mountains of Greece were very large and very beautiful.

Exercise 122.

1. Everything was announced by those who fled to the camp.
2. In the spring they will flee to the mountains of Greece.
3. We announced everything to the leaders of the cavalry.
4. Those who advise the Athenians to harm Socrates are not good citizens.
5. The slaves reported everything to the king.
6. Those who tell lies do not often deceive the king.
7. The wisest men advised the Athenians to leave their city and flee to their ships.
8. We shall equip ten ships in the spring.
9. The Athenians were the most temperate of all the Greeks.
10. The many honour those who possess most things.

Exercise 123.

1. Athenians, do not be conquered by those who fled from your fathers.
2. Deceived by the herald's words, we fitted out ships.
3. Defeated by the cavalry, we fled to the mountains.
4. The Greeks had not horses in the battle.
5. The citizens have fled and the gods have forsaken the city
6. She was more beautiful than the wife of Socrates.
7. Those who possess most things are not always the most temperate.
8. Those who had sacrificed to the gods reported many things to the general.
9. We had not a leader, and all the soldiers were perplexed.
10. The citizens, being perplexed, would not guard the walls.

SECTION V.

Grammar.—Rules for Augment in Compound Verbs:

A.M. p. 91 : R. p. 157.

Exercise 124.

1. We threw many darts into the ranks of the enemy.

2. The Greeks attacked the cavalry of the king.

3. Those who had been conquered escaped out of the city by night.

4. Having defeated the Persians, he wrote a history of the war.

5. We shall not attack the camp of the Persians.

6. Those who escaped out of the city deceived the guards.

7. The wise priest wrote a history of the Athenians.

8. Let us not attack those who saved their country.

9. Do not leave your ranks, soldiers.

10. Let us fit out ships and attack the enemy.

Exercise 125.

1. They persuaded the king to escape out of the city.
2. Having been defeated by the Persians, you wrote a history of the war.
3. All those who had sacrificed were willing to attack the enemy.
4. We do not love those who attack our walls.
5. We shall throw darts into the ranks of the Persians.
6. They will escape out of the house in three days.
7. Let us write a history of our country.
8. Those who attacked the city were defeated.
9. Do not persuade the guards to deceive their leader.
10. The ships were fitted out in the third year.

Exercise 126.

1. The Athenians attacked the army of the Persians.
2. We attacked those who had fled out of the ships.
3. Do not announce to the king the victory of the Athenians.
4. Those who had fled into the camp had not darts.
5. The city will be enslaved by those who are now attacking the walls.
6. The victory of the brave sailors was announced to the enemy.
7. Oh that those who are attacking the city may be defeated !
8. Persuade the leader to attack the camp of the enemy.
9. You fled out of the house to the harbour.
10. They wrote a history of the great war.

SECTION VI.

Grammar.—Rules for Formation and Comparison of Adverbs:
A.M. p. 52 : R. p. 54.

Exercise 127.

1. Let us quickly send away those who deceived the old man.

2. The mountains were not far distant from the river.

3. They left behind the most honourable and most temperate.

4. Many of the noblest men were sent away by the king.

5. Those who were left behind attacked the enemy bravely.

6. The cavalry fought more bravely than those drawn up before the walls.

7. Oh that the poet may act more temperately.

8. The river was not far from the enemy's camp.

9. I sent away all those who had fled to the city.

10. Those who had been trained by the rhetorician acted more wisely.

Exercise 128.

1. The bravest men do not always act most wisely.
2. The Athenians always honoured those who showed most courage.
3. We had very brave soldiers and very many darts.
4. The victory of the Athenians was quickly announced to the king.
5. All those who threw darts harmed the enemy.
6. Those who write the history of their country are honoured by all.
7. Those who had announced the victory were well treated by the citizens.
8. We shall attack the walls of the city in the winter.
9. The herald of the king has acted very wisely.
10. Let us fight very bravely and defeat the enemy.

Exercise 129.

1. The general's camp was not far distant from the city.
2. Do not send the young man away, O king !
3. Let us not leave behind in the city the women and the children.
4. The cavalry were not far distant from the enemy.
5. Do not leave your wife behind in the house.
6. The soldiers, having left their arms behind, fled quickly to the camp.
7. They left their wives and children behind in the mountains.
8. Those who had persuaded the king to attack the city fled by night.
9. The mountains of Greece were not far distant from the sea.
10. He quickly despatched a herald to the leader of the enemy.

PART IX

Section I.

Grammar.—Active of τίθημι: A.M. pp. 106, 107, 114, 115:
R. pp. 86, 87.

The Pronoun ἐγώ: A.M. p. 55: R. p. 55.

The 'Attic' Declension: A.M. p. 27: R. p. 10.

N.B.—(1) *Do not begin a sentence with any of the words—*
με, μοῦ, μοί, σέ, σοῦ, σοί.

    E.g.   *They sent me away.*
           ἀπέπεμψάν με.

(2) *Do not use the forms* με, μοῦ, μοί *after a Preposition.*

    E.g.   *He sent a herald to me.*
           ἔπεμψε πρὸς ἐμὲ κήρυκα.

(3) *A final vowel in a Preposition is usually elided before
another vowel.*

    E.g.   *from me,* ἀπ' ἐμοῦ.

    A 'hard' consonant [1] *is changed into the corresponding
aspirate before a rough breathing.*

    E.g.   *from us,* ἀφ' ἡμῶν.

Exercise 130.

1. Great were the hopes of the Athenians.
2. The herald was with me in the house.
3. Those who show most courage will conquer in the battle.
4. Those who had been set free placed their fetters in the house.
5. The general sent many gifts to me.
6. The king of the Persians enacted many laws.
7. We place the gifts in the temples.
8. They were placing the arms in the house of the general.
9. They despatched us to the camp of the Persians.
10. You were placing arms in the temple of the goddess.

[1] See A.M. p. 13, R. p. 2.

Exercise 131.

1. They placed the gifts of the citizens in the temple.
2. He was placing the arms of the general in the house of the citizen.
3. The poet will place the gift of the king in the temple.
4. He transacted the affair for me.
5. They were with me in the temple.
6. The king has enacted many laws.
7. Let us place our arms in the temple of the goddess.
8. He transacted the affairs of Greece with the wisest citizens.
9. He persuaded us to attack the walls.
10. In ten days they will announce to us the victory.

Exercise 132.

1. The conquerors despatched a herald to us on the third day.
2. The city trusted us in the terrible war.
3. Those who had been defeated fled to us by night.
4. Those who had been honoured by me would not trust the king.
5. Being perplexed, they fled out of the city to us.
6. Having left their ranks, they have fled to the Athenians.
7. The king will enact laws for the conquered.
8. We placed the arms of the general in the temple.
9. The herald was seeking us in the city.
10. Oh that the king may not enact laws for the Greeks!

Section II.

Grammar.—Middle and passive of τίθημι:

A.M. pp. 106, 107, 114, 115 : R. pp. 88, 89.

The Pronoun σύ : A.M. p. 55 : R. p. 55.

Exercise 133.

1. The enemy attacked us on the fifth day.

2. The Persians will not attack you, citizens.

3. Laws are enacted by those who administer the affairs of the city.

4. Those who were defeated will not trust you, general.

5. They transacted the affair for you.

6. We all love those who trust us.

7. Those who escaped out of the city are now with us.

8. May they not attack those who have benefited us !

9. Let us not attack those who have been left behind in the camp.

10. Those who enslave us, citizens, will enslave you.

Exercise 134.

1. They will announce to you the victory of the sailors.
2. We were with you in the mountains of Greece.
3. The general will administer the affairs most wisely with you.
4. They will attack us in the summer with the king.
5. He will be with you in Greece in the spring.
6. Those who trusted you were deceived, Demosthenes.
7. Those who threw the darts fled out of the city.
8. We despatched a herald to you, O king, on the third day.
9. Many laws were enacted by us on behalf of the city.
10. He persuaded us to attack the walls by night.

Exercise 135.

1. Those who love their country will not trust you.
2. The cavalry of the enemy will not attack us.
3. Those who enslave us will enslave Greece.
4. The younger men believed you, Socrates.
5. Those who honour the gods obey those who enact laws.
6. The slaves fled to us by night.
7. Oh that you may not defeat us in the battle!
8. Those who were left in the camp were braver than the generals.
9. A large army was sent by us into Greece.
10. Those who harmed us have not benefited their country.

SECTION III.

Grammar.—Active of ἵστημι : A.M. pp. 110, 111, 114, 115 :
R. pp. 90, 91.

The Oblique Cases of αὐτός : A.M. p. 56 : R. p. 57

Rule.—αὐτός **used by itself in the oblique cases =** *Latin* eum,
eam, id, etc., *him, her, it.* In this sense do not
place the Pronoun first in the sentence.

We loosed them.

ἐλύσαμεν αὐτούς.

Exercise 136.

1. Having defeated the Persians, the Athenians set up a
   trophy.

2. The boy is standing in the broad road.

3. We wrote many letters to him in the summer.

4. The conquered will not set up a trophy.

5. The king despatched him to the leader of the Greeks.

6. The guards stood in front of the gates of the city.

7. The general is setting up a trophy in the island.

8. All the Athenians honoured and loved him.

9. We ordered him to place his arms in the temple.

10. Having prospered in the war, we set up a trophy.

Exercise 137.

1. We announced to him the victory of the general.
2. Those standing in the road were not far distant from the camp.
3. The general set up a trophy in the temple of the goddess.
4. The laws of the city are not enacted by him.
5. We stood with him in front of the walls.
6. Those who conquer the enemy often set up trophies.
7. We trusted both you and him in the war.
8. The Athenians will be willing to despatch you to the king.
9. You stood with me in the road.
10. We sought him in the mountains of Greece.

Exercise 138.

1. Let us set up a trophy in the island, Demosthenes.
2. Persuaded by Socrates, we trained him in wisdom.
3. The king was with him in the camp.
4. We stood with you in the road.
5. The task will be very difficult for you, citizens.
6. Oh that the Persians may not set up a trophy in the island !
7. Do not persuade him to fly out of the city.
8. The sharp teeth of the lion will not harm him.
9. Every city despatched heralds to the king.
10. Those who had left their ranks had not horses.

SECTION IV.

Grammar.—Middle and passive of ἵστημι :

A.M. pp. 106, 107, 114, 115 : R. pp. 92, 93.

N.B.—*Use the Article before Possessive Pronouns.*

E.g. *My father.*

ὁ ἐμὸς πατήρ.

Exercise 139.

1. They revolted from the Athenians in the summer.

2. Trophies are not set up by the conquered.

3. My father ordered him to cease from the task.

4. We shall not revolt from you, Athenians.

5. My arms were in the camp.

6. The island has revolted from the Athenians.

7. You revolted from the king of the Persians.

8. My house was not far distant from the sea.

9. Having revolted from the Athenians, they were perplexed.

10. My father placed the arms in the temple.

Exercise 140.

1. The boy was trained in wisdom by my mother.
2. The old men persuaded us to revolt.
3. Those who revolted were drawn up in the road.
4. My brother wrote a history of the great war.
5. My wife wrote a letter to her mother.
6. My son was persuaded by the pleasant words of the orator.
7. The bravest soldiers revolted from the king.
8. My father was the most temperate of all the Greeks.
9. They will write a letter to you, father.
10. He is standing with my son in front of the house.

Exercise 141.

1. The most temperate men will not revolt from the king.
2. The general ordered me to stand in front of the walls.
3. Those who ask for arms will not flee from the enemy.
4. My father announced the victory of the Athenians.
5. My mother was very rich and had many houses.
6. The mountains of my country were beautiful with trees.
7. Those who stood with me in the road were fighting very bravely.
8. Having defeated the Persians, he is setting up a trophy.
9. He who trusts kings is often deceived.
10. My father will be with you in three days.

SECTION V.

Grammar.—Active of δίδωμι : A.M. pp. 112-115 :

R. pp. 44, 94, 95.

Exercise 142.

1. They gave us many horses and large houses.

2. They used to give many presents to the soldiers.

3. He gave me the lion's body.

4. We shall give everything to those who save the city.

5. The gods gave the victory to us.

6. Always give to those who ask.

7. Your father ordered me to obey the laws.

8. Socrates, persuade your son to honour his mother.

9. We all trusted your father in the battle.

10. The judge was persuaded by gifts to set your brother free.

Exercise 143.

1. We placed all our arms in the house.
2. Your father set up a trophy in the island.
3. They had the courage of their father.
4. May the citizens give you many gifts!
5. The Athenians did not then honour kings.
6. Your house was far distant from the river.
7. Let us give arms to those left behind in the camp.
8. I gave all the arms to the slaves.
9. Your mother, being perplexed, despatched me to the king.
10. Do not ask for many things : give everything.

Exercise 144.

1. All the cities revolted from the king.
2. We gave many beautiful presents to the judge.
3. The horses were more useful to us than the slaves.
4. It will not be very honourable to give everything to the enemy.
5. The judge was more temperate than the poet.
6. They are giving everything to their brothers.
7. I was with him in Greece for many months.
8. There were many sailors with us in the harbour.
9. Do not give gifts to free citizens.
10. Most true were the words of my mother.

SECTION VI.

Grammar.—Middle and Passive of δίδωμι :

A.M. pp. 112-115 : R. pp. 96, 97.

Exercise 145.

1. Many gifts were given to us by our fathers.

2. The general betrayed the city to the enemy.

3. Your brother will not betray his country.

4. You were saved by the valour of our fathers.

5. Those who were perplexed always fled to our city.

6. The city was betrayed by the guards.

7. We do not give everything to those who ask.

8. The houses were given to me by my brother.

9. Our city will be betrayed by the guards.

10. All those who honour the gods love our temples.

Exercise 146.

1. Give arms to the slaves and guard the house.
2. The king was saved together with those who had fled.
3. Let us not betray those who have fled to us.
4. Many gifts are given to those who conquer in the contest.
5. Arms were given to those who had fled out of the city.
6. Oh that the city may not be betrayed!
7. Do not give the horse to your brother.
8. Our fathers revolted from the Persians.
9. He wrote a history of our country.
10. They despatched a herald to our king.

Exercise 147.

1. Do not attack our city, O king!
2. Those who harm our country are not loved by the gods.
3. The city will place all its hope in our courage.
4. In the spring our island is beautiful with trees.
5. Do not betray those who trusted you, O king!
6. Let us not betray our city to the nobles.
7. The bravest soldiers were with us in the city.
8. They despatched me with my brother to Greece.
9. Our soldiers ceased from the battle.
10. Those who betrayed the city are standing in the road.

SECTION VII.

Grammar.—The Verb δείκνυμι : A.M. pp. 114, 115 : R. p. 99.

The Verb εἰμί : A.M. pp. 118, 124 : R. pp. 98, 183.

Full Conjugation of εἰμί : A.M. pp. 117, 118 : R. pp. 63, 64.

N.B.—The Verb ἔρχομαι is only used in the Present Indicative in Attic : thus the Paradigms of 'I come,' 'I go,' in common use are as follows :

Present—ἔρχομαι, ἦα, ἴω, ἴοιμι, ἴθι, ἰέναι, ἰών.

Future—εἶμι, ἴοιμι, ἰέναι, ἰών.

Aorist—ἦλθον, ἔλθω, ἔλθοιμι, ἐλθέ, ἐλθεῖν, ἐλθών.

Exercise 148.

1. The conquerors are coming to the city.

2. We went to the mountains of Greece.

3. Those who are in the city will be defeated.

4. Let us go to the camp of the Persians.

5. Oh that your city may always be free, Athenians !

6. He came with us to the king.

7. After the battle we shall go to the harbour.

8. The soldier will go to our city.

9. Be brave in the battle, soldiers.

10. He was appointed general by the king.

Exercise 149.

1. After the victory the Athenians appointed Demosthenes general.
2. Having come into the house he gave me the arms.
3. We persuaded the king to go into Greece.
4. May you be more brave than your father!
5. May you not go with the king to the island!
6. Those who fled out of the city will go to you.
7. The law was enacted on behalf of those who come to our city.
8. Let us go to the land and hunt lions.
9. Oh that you may be wiser than the judge!
10. Having come into the island they set up a trophy.

Exercise 150.

1. Let us go to him on the third day.
2. They will go to Greece with those who conquered in the battle.
3. After the war they went to all the cities of Greece.
4. We came to the city on the tenth day.
5. He ordered the herald to go to the king.
6. The ships, having come into the harbour, were safe.
7. They came to Greece with those who revolted.
8. The king gave the city to the Athenians.
9. Having enacted many laws he went out of the city.
10. Not being very brave they do not honour courage.

PART X

SECTION I.

Grammar.—The Pronoun οὗτος : A.M. p. 57 : R. p. 56.

Rule.—οὗτος and ἐκεῖνος, *when used with nouns, require the*
article, but **they must not come between the**
article and the noun.

> *E.g.   These gifts.*
> ταῦτα τὰ δῶρα.
> *or* τὰ δῶρα ταῦτα.

Exercise 151.

1. All men admired this city.
2. Those who honour virtue will admire Socrates.
3. The cavalry fought most bravely for Greece.
4. The victory of Demosthenes increased the honour of the city.
5. These gifts were pleasing to the king.
6. Your father always admired this city.
7. It will be difficult for the cavalry to fight in these mountains.
8. These poets were admired by all the citizens.
9. The Greeks gave many beautiful gifts to this general.
10. These women will fight for their country.

Exercise 152.

1. All men honoured the courage of this woman.
2. Those who admire the Greeks often go to Greece.
3. Those who displayed courage increased the honour of their country.
4. This city admired poets and orators.
5. These boys went to the mountains at night.
6. This horse was given to me by my brother.
7. After this battle many were enslaved by the king.
8. The citizens will admire those who fight well.
9. These sailors betrayed their city to the enemy.
10. In this island there are many beautiful trees.

Exercise 153.

1. Let us not admire those who betrayed their country.
2. The sons of the king increased the honour of the city.
3. This woman had three brothers.
4. Do not admire those who tell lies.
5. Do not set up a trophy in this island.
6. Every city will admire our courage.
7. These ships came into the harbour by night.
8. For four days these soldiers were in the camp.
9. These things will not be difficult for a clever boy.
10. This army was defeated by those who had revolted.

SECTION II.

Grammar.—The Pronoun ἐκεῖνος : A.M. p. 57 : R. p. 56.

N.B.—The Paradigm of εἶπον, '*I said,*' *is as follows* :

εἶπον, εἴπω, εἴποιμι, εἰπέ, εἰπεῖν, εἰπών.

The forms in use in Attic for the Indicative are:

εἶπον, εἶπας, εἶπε, εἴπατον, εἰπάτην, εἴπομεν,
εἴπατε, εἶπον.

Exercise 154.

1. The soldiers marched into that city on the third day.

2. We shall remain in the camp with the general.

3. After the battle the citizens gave gifts to the soldiers.

4. All the ships remained in the harbour.

5. Those who reported the victory said this.

6. Let us not say this to those who betrayed the city.

7. We shall not say this to the boy's father.

8. Those who had come to the city told us this.

9. Having said this they went to the walls of the city.

10. We marched with the king for ten days.

Exercise 155.

1. The cavalry were drawn up in that road.
2. The judge was persuaded to say that.
3. Do not say that to the citizens, Demosthenes.
4. Having said that, he ceased from his speech.
5. The king told me this on the second day.
6. The boy did not tell his mother this.
7. Having marched to the city, we shall announce this.
8. In that island women received much honour.
9. It will be easy to increase the honour of this city.
10. Your words were very true and more temperate than mine.

Exercise 156.

1. Let us not injure those who said this.
2. After this the richest men came to the king.
3. Those left in the city remained in their houses.
4. You will flee from us, Socrates.
5. May you not be deceived of your hope !
6. Having equipped many ships, the Athenians ordered the herald to go.
7. That man will not admire the mountains of Greece.
8. Your father told me this.
9. Go with your brother to the gates.
10. You will stay in the city, soldiers, and fight very bravely.

Section III.

Grammar.—The Pronoun αὐτός : A.M. p. 56 : R. p. 55.

Rule.—**Used in the Nominative by itself, or used with Nouns (or Pronouns) in any Case,** αὐτός = *Latin* ipse, *self*. In this sense it must not come between the Article and the Noun.

> *I myself said this.*
> αὐτὸς εἶπον τοῦτο.
> *The man himself came.*
> ὁ ἀνὴρ αὐτὸς ⎱
> or αὐτός ὁ ἀνὴρ ⎰ ἦλθεν.

N.B.—(1) Remember that the complement of the verb γίγνομαι, *I become*, follows the same rules as those given on p. 16 for the complement of εἰμί.

> *He became the leader.*
> ἡγεμὼν ἐγένετο.

(2) ἀποθνήσκω is used as the passive of ἀποκτείνω.

> *He was killed by his brother.*
> ἀπέθανεν ὑπὸ τοῦ ἀδελφοῦ.

Exercise 157.

1. We wished to send them to the king himself.
2. Slaves do not often become poets.
3. We killed those who had betrayed the city.
4. Those who came to the city were killed.
5. We ourselves will kill those who revolt.
6. The king will die in three days.
7. They killed the general himself.
8. He himself will kill those who fly.
9. Those who escaped out of the city were killed.
10. The boy died in the night.

Exercise 158.

1. Those who remain will be killed by the guards.
2. Having received many gifts, he died.
3. He said this to the general himself.
4. We will not become slaves.
5. He himself was killed by the Athenians.
6. You yourselves wished to hunt the lion.
7. Demosthenes did not persuade the citizens themselves.
8. You will be killed by the guards of the city.
9. The poet will not become a general.
10. Socrates himself will not say that.

Exercise 159.

1. May you become more wise than your father?
2. Do not kill those who have benefited the city.
3. Let us not march against the king himself.
4. After this she herself wished to go.
5. We shall kill all those who are in the house.
6. The general himself was killed by you.
7. He himself came with me to the mountain.
8. You yourself were deceived by pleasing words.
9. The gods themselves gave us this country.
10. Let us remain in the city ourselves.

SECTION IV.

Rule.—αὐτός immediately preceded by the Article
= *Latin* idem, *the same.*

The same man said this.

ὁ αὐτὸς ἀνὴρ εἶπε τοῦτο.

Exercise 160.

1. The herald arrived on the fourth night.

2. The city itself was destroyed by the enemy.

3. We shall arrive at the city in five days.

4. He destroyed all the ships of the Athenians.

5. Let us not destroy the walls of the city.

6. Many gifts were sent to us by the same man.

7. The ships arrive in the harbour on the same day.

8. The enemy destroyed the great walls.

9. They will arrive at the same city in four months.

10. Everything was destroyed by those who had revolted.

Exercise 161.

1. Having arrived at the city, he announced the victory.
2. This general will not conquer the king of the Persians.
3. They were not willing to obey the same leaders.
4. The guards themselves were killed by the enemy.
5. Socrates did not corrupt the young men in the city.
6. Do not destroy the walls of your city, Athenians.
7. Demosthenes himself persuaded them to march.
8. The same soldiers attacked the city by night.
9. The king himself was not far distant from the cavalry.
10. After three days the general arrived with the same army.

Exercise 162.

1. Those who write many things do not always become poets.
2. Having destroyed the city, he wished to kill all the citizens.
3. Having arrived in Greece, he wished to go to the mountains.
4. The same man betrayed the city to the enemy.
5. Having come to the island, he despatched a herald.
6. Our city will not receive your laws.
7. The same woman told us this.
8. We ourselves do not all admire the same things.
9. Those who arrived at the city announced the same things.
10. We were all deceived by the same orator.

Section V.

Grammar.—The Verbs λαμβάνω, ὁρῶ, :

A.M. pp. 126, 128 : R. pp. 174, 184.

Exercise 163.

1. We took the city on the fourth day.

2. We shall not see the king himself.

3. They saw the same woman in the road.

4. We see many beautiful trees in the island.

5. We shall take the city in three days.

6. Having arrived at the temple he saw the same priest.

7. Good judges do not take gifts.

8. May we not see our city destroyed !

9. You will not see those who killed the king.

10. Do not march into Greece with the same army.

Exercise 164.

1. We did not see those who had destroyed the walls.
2. We shall see the same women in the temple.
3. The bravest sailors do not often become poets.
4. Having taken the city, he arrived with the same army.
5. Socrates himself did not wish to see him.
6. We shall say the same things to the soldiers and the sailors.
7. Those who saw the king admired his courage.
8. Let us take the city and set up a trophy.
9. The wisest men do not always say the same things.
10. Having taken the city, they gave it to the Athenians.

Exercise 165.

1. Having arrived in the island they fought most bravely.
2. Those who take gifts do not always honour those who give them.
3. The poet spoke more wisely than the orator.
4. We wished to ask for very many things.
5. Those who took arms were killed by the guards.
6. Having seen the temples we shall not remain in the city.
7. Those who see the goddess will die.
8. The same general saw us in the island.
9. Those cities were destroyed by the same soldier.
10. We shall kill those who betrayed the city.

GREEK-ENGLISH EXERCISES

(The numbers in brackets after the number of each exercise indicate the exercises in the preceding part to which it corresponds.)

I. (Ex. 1-3).

1. ἐν ταῖς τῆς μούσης χώραις.

2. λύετε τὴν μοῦσαν.

3. παύει τὰς μάχας.

4. λύω τὰς τῆς θεᾶς πέδας.

5. παύουσι τὴν μάχην.

6. λύομεν τὰς θεάς.

7. ἡ τῶν μουσῶν ἀρετή.

8. παύει τὴν μάχην ἐν τῇ χώρᾳ.

9. λύομεν θεάν.

10. παύομεν μάχην.

II. (Ex. 4-6).

1. κωλύσομεν τὴν θεάν.
2. θηρεύσουσι τὴν σοφίαν καὶ τὴν ἀρετήν.
3. ἐν τῇ οἰκίᾳ λύσω τὰς πέδας.
4. θηρεύομεν ἐν τῇ χώρᾳ.
5. ἡ θεὰ παύει τὴν μάχην.
6. κωλύετε τὴν τῆς στρατιᾶς νίκην.
7. θηρεύσετε τὴν ἀρετήν.
8. ἡ στρατιὰ παύσει τὴν μάχην.
9. θηρεύσομεν τὴν τιμήν.
10. λύσετε τὰς πέδας.

III. (Ex. 7-9).

1. ὁ ταμίας ἐκώλυε τὴν νίκην.
2. ἐπαύομεν τὴν μάχην.
3. ἐθηρεύετε τὴν ἀρετὴν καὶ τὴν σοφίαν.
4. λύσομεν τὰς τοῦ κριτοῦ πέδας.
5. ὁ νεανίας θηρεύσει ἐν τῇ χώρᾳ.
6. ἐλύομεν τὰς πέδας ἐν τῇ οἰκίᾳ.
7. παιδεύσεις τοὺς νεανίας ἐν τῇ σοφίᾳ.
8. ἐθηρεύομεν τὴν σοφίαν ἐκ τῆς χώρας.
9. οἱ κριταὶ ἐπαίδευον τοὺς πολίτας.
10. ὁ πολίτης ἔπαυε τὴν μάχην.

IV. (Ex. 10-12).

1. ὁ ναύτης ἐθήρευσε τὸν στρατιώτην ἐκ τῆς οἰκίας.
2. ἐπαίδευσε τὸν ναύτην ἐν τῇ σοφίᾳ.
3. ἐπαίδευσαν τοὺς νεανίας καὶ τοὺς στρατιώτας.
4. ἐκώλυσαν τὴν τῆς θεᾶς νίκην.
5. οἱ ναῦται ἔπαυσαν τὰς μάχας.
6. οἱ στρατιῶται θηρεύουσι τὴν ἀρετήν.
7. ὁ κριτὴς θηρεύσει ἐν τῇ χώρᾳ.
8. οἱ νεανίαι κωλύσουσι τὴν τῶν πολιτῶν νίκην.
9. οἱ κριταὶ παύσουσι τὴν μάχην.
10. ἐθήρευσαν ἐν τῇ τῆς θεᾶς χώρᾳ.

V. (Ex. 13-15).

1. πεπαίδευκας τοὺς πολίτας, ὦ κριτά.
2. οἱ ἄνθρωποι θηρεύσουσι τὴν ἀρετήν.
3. ὁ στρατηγὸς κεκώλυκε τὴν νίκην.
4. λελύκαμεν τοὺς ναύτας καὶ τοὺς στρατιώτας.
5. πεπαίδευκε τοὺς νεανίας ἐν τῇ σοφίᾳ.
6. ὁ στρατιώτης λέλυκε τὸν ναύτην.
7. οἱ τῶν στρατηγῶν λόγοι παύσουσι τὴν μάχην.
8. ὁ πόλεμος λύσει τοὺς πολίτας.
9. τοῖς λόγοις κεκώλυκας τὴν νίκην, ὦ κριτά.
10. οὐ πεπαιδεύκαμεν τοὺς νεανίας ἐν τῷ πολέμῳ.

VI. (Ex. 16-18).

1. ἐλελύκεσαν τὸν τοῦ κριτοῦ δοῦλον.
2. ἐσεσείκεσαν τὰ ὅπλα ἐν τῇ μάχῃ.
3. ὁ στρατηγὸς ἐκεκρούκει τὸν δοῦλον.
4. τοῖς λόγοις ἐκεκωλύκη τὸν πόλεμον.
5. ἐλελύκης τοὺς στρατιώτας καὶ τοὺς ναύτας.
6. ὁ πόλεμος κωλύσει τὸ ἔργον.
7. τὰ τῆς θεᾶς δῶρά ἐστιν ἐν τῇ οἰκίᾳ.
8. ἔστι δένδρα ἐν ταῖς χώραις.
9. τοῖς ἔργοις κεκωλύκασι τὸν πόλεμον.
10. ὁ ἵππος ἐστιν ἐν τῷ ποταμῷ.

VII. (Ex. 19-21).

1. ὁ σοφὸς κριτὴς παιδεύσει τὸν νεανίαν.
2. οἱ στρατιῶται πιστεύουσι τοῖς στρατηγοῖς ἐν τῇ μάχῃ.
3. ἐκρούσαμεν τὴν τοῦ σοφοῦ νεανίου κεφαλήν.
4. οἱ ἀγαθοὶ δοῦλοι παιδεύουσι τὸν ἵππον.
5. τὰ τοῦ στρατιώτου ὅπλα ἐστιν ἐν τῇ οἰκίᾳ.
6. οἱ φίλιοι στρατιῶταί εἰσιν ἐν τῷ στρατοπέδῳ.
7. ἐθηρεύσαμεν τοὺς ἀνθρώπους εἰς τὴν ὁδόν.
8. οἱ τοῦ κριτοῦ λόγοι σοφοί εἰσίν.
9. θηρεύει τὸν ναύτην πρὸς τὰς πύλας.
10. τὰ τῆς θεᾶς ὅπλα ἐστιν ἐν τῷ ποταμῷ.

VIII. (Ex. 22-24).

1. ὁ τοῦ κριτοῦ ἀδελφὸς οὐ ποιητὴς ἦν.
2. ἦμεν ἐν τῇ τῆς θεᾶς χώρᾳ.
3. οἱ στρατηγοὶ χρήσιμοι ἦσαν ἐν τῷ πολέμῳ.
4. οἱ ἀγαθοὶ κριταὶ πιστεύουσι τοῖς νόμοις.
5. οἱ τοῦ κριτοῦ λόγοι χρήσιμοί εἰσιν.
6. πολλάκις κωλύει μάχην ἐν τῇ νήσῳ.
7. ὁ στρατηγὸς φίλιος ἦν τῷ ἀγαθῷ κριτῇ.
8. ὁ ποταμὸς χρήσιμός ἐστι τοῖς πολίταις.
9. ἡ ὁδὸς χρησίμη ἦν τοῖς στρατιώταις.
10. τὰ τοῦ ἀνθρώπου ὅπλα ἐν τῷ ποταμῷ ἦν.

IX. (Ex. 25-27).

1. τὰ ἔργα χαλεπὰ ἔσται τῷ κριτῇ.
2. ἡ θεὰ σείσει τὴν γῆν.
3. χαλεπὸν ἔσται πιστεύειν τῷ δούλῳ.
4. καλὸς ἔσται ὁ τοῦ κριτοῦ λόγος.
5. ἡ τῶν στρατηγῶν σοφία χρησίμη ἦν ἐν τῇ μάχῃ.
6. οὐ πολλάκις ἐν τῇ νήσῳ ἦν.
7. οἱ αἰσχροὶ δοῦλοι οὐκ ἦσαν ἐν τῇ οἰκίᾳ.
8. οἱ πολῖται οὐκ ἐλεύθεροι ἔσονται.
9. αἱ τῶν ἵππων κεφαλαὶ καλαί εἰσιν.
10. ἡ γλῶττα πολλάκις χρησίμη ἐστιν.

X. (Ex. 28-30).

1. λύσομεν τοὺς ἀνδρείους δούλους.
2. οἱ ἀγαθοὶ κριταὶ ἐπίστευσαν τοῖς νόμοις.
3. ἡ σοφὴ θεὰ ἐπίστευσε τῷ ἀνθρώπῳ.
4. οὐ λελύκαμεν τοὺς ἵππους.
5. ὁ κριτὴς πολλάκις κρούσει τὸν αἰσχρὸν δοῦλον.
6. αἱ τῶν ἵππων κεφαλαὶ αἰσχραὶ ἦσαν.
7. τοῖς σοφοῖς λόγοις παύσομεν τὴν μάχην.
8. χαλεπὸν ἔσται παιδεύειν τὸν αἰσχρὸν δοῦλον.
9. τὰ ἔργα χαλεπὰ ἔσται τῷ ἀνθρώπῳ.
10. ταμίαι ἐσόμεθα τῆς χώρας.

XI. (Ex. 31-33).

1. ὁ φύλαξ ἐπίστευσε τῷ κήρυκι.
2. τάξομεν τοὺς στρατιώτας ἐν τῇ μάχῃ.
3. οἱ πολῖται οὐκ ἔπραξαν τὰ τῆς νήσου.
4. οἱ κήρυκες κακῶς πράξουσιν ἐν τῇ ὁδῷ.
5. κακῶς πεπράχαμεν τὰ τῶν νήσων.
6. τέταχε τοὺς στρατιώτας ἐν τῇ ὁδῷ.
7. ἔταξαν τοὺς ναύτας ἐν ταῖς ὁδοῖς.
8. ἐκελεύσαμεν τὸν στρατηγὸν πράττειν τὰ τῶν νήσων.
9. ὁ κριτὴς οὐ πιστεύσει τῷ κήρυκι.
10. ὁ στρατηγὸς εὖ ἔπραττεν ἐν τοῖς πολέμοις.

XII. (Ex. 34-36).

1. κήρυκας ἔπεμψε πρὸς τὰς νήσους.
2. ἐκελεύσαμεν τοὺς στρατηγοὺς πέμπειν δῶρα.
3. πεπόμφαμεν καλὰ δῶρα πρὸς τοὺς ναύτας.
4. ἡ θεὰ κακῶς πράξει ἐν τῷ πολέμῳ.
5. ὁ ποιητὴς πέμψει δῶρον πρὸς τὸν στρατηγόν.
6. ὁ κριτὴς ἔσται ἐν τῷ στρατοπέδῳ.
7. πέμψει ἵππους πρὸς τοὺς κριτάς.
8. πέμψεις κήρυκα εἰς τὸ στρατόπεδον.
9. πέπομφε κήρυκα πρὸς τὰς πύλας.
10. πέμψει τὸν ἀνδρεῖον στρατιώτην πρὸς τὸν στρατηγόν

XIII. (Ex. 37-39).

1. τῇ ἀρετῇ ἐσώσαμεν τὴν πατρίδα.
2. ἐκέλευσε τὸν δοῦλον σῴζειν τὸ δένδρον.
3. χαλεπὸν ἔσται πιστεύειν τοῖς γέρουσιν.
4. ὁ νεανίας ἐκέλευσε τὸν δοῦλον σῴζειν τὰ ὅπλα.
5. σώσομεν τὴν πατρίδα ἐκ δείνου πολέμου.
6. κελεύσομεν τοὺς δούλους θηρεύειν τὸν λέοντα.
7. ὁ τοῦ κριτοῦ ἀδελφὸς σώσει τοὺς νόμους.
8. πείθουσι τὸν δοῦλον λύειν τὰς πέδας.
9. πέπεικας τοὺς κριτὰς παιδεύειν τὸν νεανίαν.
10. οὐ πείσεις τὸν γέροντα, ὦ δοῦλε.

XIV. (Ex. 40-42).

1. πιστεύσομεν τῷ ἡγεμόνι τέτταρας ἡμέρας.

2. τῇ τρίτῃ ἡμέρᾳ ἐθήρευσαν τοὺς κήρυκας ἐκ τῆς νήσου.

3. ἦμεν ἐν τῇ χώρᾳ ἑπτὰ μῆνας.

4. τῇ δεκάτῃ ἡμέρᾳ δῶρα πέμψει πρὸς τοὺς κριτάς.

5. δέκα ἡμέρας ἔσονται ἐν τῇ νήσῳ.

6. εὖ πράξει τὰ τῶν νήσων ἑπτὰ μῆνας.

7. δεινὸς ἔσται ὁ ἀγὼν τοῖς ἀνδρείοις νεανίαις.

8. τὰ τοῦ στρατιώτου ὅπλα ἦν ἐν τῇ οἰκίᾳ ἓξ ἡμέρας.

9. ὀκτὼ μῆνας ἔσωσαν τὰς τοῦ κριτοῦ ἐπιστολάς.

10. ἐκέλευσε τὸν δοῦλον νυκτὸς πράττειν τὸ πρᾶγμα.

XV. (Ex. 43-45).

1. οὐ λύσονται τὸν Δημοσθένη οἱ πολῖται.

2. οἱ εὔφρονες στρατηγοὶ λύσονται τοὺς ἀνδρείους στρατιώτας.

3. οὐκ ἀληθεῖς ἦσαν οἱ τοῦ Δημοσθένους λόγοι.

4. ἐπείσαμεν τοὺς νεανίας νυκτὸς θηρεύειν τὸν λέοντα.

5. χαλεπὸν ἔσται τὰ τῶν ἡγεμόνων πράττειν.

6. ἐπιστολὰς ἐγράψαμεν πρὸς τὸν εὔφρονα γέροντα.

7. πείθουσι τοὺς εὐγενεῖς γράφειν ἐπιστολάς.

8. τεττάρων μηνῶν λυσόμεθα τὸν γέροντα.

9. ἐπιστολὰς πέμψουσι πρὸς τοὺς εὐγενεῖς.

10. οἱ ἀγαθοὶ δοῦλοι λύσονται τὸν νεανίαν.

XVI. (Ex. 46-48).

1. οὐκ ἀληθεῖς ἦσαν οἱ τῶν Ἑλλήνων λόγοι.
2. τῇ ἕκτῃ ἡμέρᾳ ἐπαύσαντο τῆς μάχης.
3. ἔπεμψαν πέντε ἐπιστολὰς πρὸς τὸν Δημοσθένη.
4. ἐλύσαντο τοὺς ἀγαθοὺς φύλακας καὶ τοὺς ἀνδρείους δούλους.
5. οὐκ ἐλύσατο τὸν ποιητὴν ὁ στρατηγός.
6. ἀληθεῖς ἔσονται οἱ τοῦ ἀγαθοῦ δούλου λόγοι.
7. τὸ τῶν ποιητῶν γένος οὐ φίλιον ἦν τοῖς δούλοις.
8. ἔστι τρία γένη τῶν Ἑλλήνων.
9. παύσονται τοῦ δεινοῦ πολέμου τεττάρων μηνῶν.
10. πέντε ἐτῶν οὐκ ἔσονται λέοντες ἐν τῇ χώρᾳ.

XVII. (Ex. 49-51).

1. ὁ νεανίας λέλυται τοὺς δούλους.
2. οἱ γέροντες ἐλέλυντο τὸν φύλακα.
3. δεινὴ ἔσται ἡ τῆς πόλεως δύναμις
4. αἱ πόλεις οὐ φίλιαι ἦσαν τοῖς κήρυξιν.
5. λελύμεθα τοὺς ἀνδρείους φύλακας.
6. οἱ εὐγενεῖς παύσονται τῶν ἀγώνων.
7. ἐλελύμεθα τοὺς χρησίμους δούλους.
8. ἡ μάχη παύσεται τῇ πρώτῃ ἡμέρᾳ.
9. ἐλέλυτο τοὺς τῆς πόλεως φύλακας.
10. ἔπεμψαν τοὺς γέροντας πρὸς τὰς τῆς πόλεως πύλας.

XVIII. (Ex. 52-54).

1. ἐλύθησαν οἱ ἀνδρεῖοι δοῦλοι ὑπὸ τοῦ στρατηγοῦ.
2. ἐλύθημεν ὑπὸ τῶν στρατιωτῶν.
3. οὐκ εὐρεῖαι ἦσαν αἱ τῆς νήσου ὁδοί.
4. ἐλύθης ὑπὸ τῶν πολιτῶν, ὦ Δημόσθενες.
5. οἱ τοῦ στρατιώτου λόγοι ἡδεῖς ἔσονται τῷ στρα-τηγῷ.
6. πέντε μηνῶν λύσομεθα τὸν τοῦ ἡγεμόνος ἀδελφόν.
7. ἡδὺ ἔσται γράφειν ἐπιστολὰς πρὸς τὸν Σωκράτη.
8. ἡ μάχη ἐκωλύθη ὑπὸ τοῦ νεανίου.
9. ἦσαν καλοὶ ἰχθύες ἐν τῷ εὐρεῖ ποταμῷ.
10. ὁ εὔφρων πολίτης ἔπεισε τὸν δοῦλον δῶρα πέμπειν πρὸς τὸν κριτήν.

XIX. (Ex. 55-57).

1. λυθησόμεθα ὑπὸ τοῦ Δημοσθένους.
2. ὁ γέρων λυθήσεται ὑπὸ τοῦ βασιλέως.
3. εὖ πράττει τὰ πράγματα τῷ βασιλεῖ.
4. οἱ ἱππῆς λυθήσονται ὑπὸ τῶν στρατηγῶν.
5. κωλυθησόμεθα τοῖς τοῦ ποιητοῦ σοφοῖς λόγοις.
6. οἱ ἡγεμόνες εὖ ἔταξαν τοὺς ἱππέας ἐν τῇ ὁδῷ.
7. χαλεπὸν ἔσται πείθειν τοὺς βασιλέας.
8. χρήσιμα ἦν τὰ ὅπλα τοῖς Πέρσαις ἐν τῇ μάχῃ.
9. κωλυθήσονται ὑπὸ τῶν τοῦ βασιλέως στρατιωτῶν.
10. αἱ τοῦ ναύτου πέδαι ἐλύθησαν ὑπὸ τοῦ δούλου.

XX. (Ex. 58-60).

1. ἐτιμῶμεν τοὺς τοῦ σοφοῦ ποιητοῦ λόγους.
2. τιμᾶται ὑπὸ τῶν τοῦ βασιλέως φυλάκων.
3. τιμώμεθα ὑπὸ τῶν σοφῶν γερόντων.
4. ὁ βασιλεὺς δώροις ἐτίμα τοὺς σοφοὺς παῖδας.
5. οἱ τῆς πόλεως νόμοι οὐκ ἐτιμῶντο ὑπὸ τῶν ῥητόρων.
6. οἱ θεοὶ ἀγῶσιν ἐτιμῶντο ὑπὸ τῶν Ἑλλήνων.
7. ἐτιμῶ ὑπὸ τοῦ βασιλέως, ὦ ποιητά.
8. οἱ σοφοὶ ποιηταὶ ἀεὶ ἐτιμῶντο ἐν ταῖς πόλεσιν.
9. ἐτίμων τοὺς τῆς πόλεως ἀνδρείους φύλακας.
10. τιμᾷ ὑπὸ τῶν ῥητόρων καὶ τῶν ποιητῶν.

XXI. (Ex. 61-63).

1. ἡ πόλις ἐφιλεῖτο ὑπὸ τῶν ἀνδρείων πολιτῶν.
2. αἱ μητέρες ἐφίλουν τοὺς παῖδας.
3. οἱ πατέρες ἐν τοῖς λόγοις ἐτίμων τὸν ῥήτορα.
4. οἱ τοῦ βασιλέως παῖδες εὖ ἐποίουν τὴν πόλιν.
5. τοῖς ἔργοις εὖ ποιοῦμεν τὴν πατρίδα.
6. φιλοῦσι καὶ τιμῶσι τὸν πατέρα καὶ τὴν μητέρα.
7. εὖ ποιεῖ ὑπὸ τοῦ ἀνδρείου στρατηγοῦ.
8. κακῶς ἐποίουν τοὺς ναύτας καὶ τοὺς στρατιώτας.
9. ἡδὺ ἔσται τῷ βασιλεῖ τὸ τοῦ παιδὸς δῶρον.
10. πέντε μηνῶν παυσόμεθα τοῦ ἀγῶνος.

XXII. (Ex. 64-66).

1. τοῖς ἔργοις ἐδηλοῦμεν τὴν ἀρετήν.
2. οἱ ἀγαθοὶ ἄνδρες οὐ δουλοῦσι τοὺς ἀδελφούς.
3. ὁ ποιητὴς φιλεῖται ὑπὸ τῶν ἐλευθέρων πολιτῶν.
4. οὐ φιλεῖ ὑπὸ τῶν στρατιωτῶν, ὦ στρατηγέ.
5. οὐ δηλοῦτε τὴν ἀρετήν, ὦ ἄνδρες.
6. δουλοῦμεν ἄνδρες ἄνδρα, καὶ πόλεις πόλιν.
7. τοῖς ἔργοις δηλοῦται ἡ τῶν στρατηγῶν ἀρετή.
8. ἡ μήτηρ οὐκ ἐπίστευσε τοῖς τοῦ ἀνδρὸς λόγοις.
9. ὁ ῥήτωρ δηλοῖ τὴν ἀρετὴν καὶ τὴν σοφίαν.
10. αἱ πόλεις ἐδουλοῦντο ὑπὸ τῶν Περσῶν.

XXIII. (Ex. 67-69).

1. ἦσαν μέλαιναι νῆες ἐν τῷ εὐρεῖ ποταμῷ.
2. τοῖς ἔργοις δηλώσομεν τὴν ἀρετήν.
3. τοῖς ἀγῶσι τιμήσομεν τοὺς θεούς.
4. φιλήσομεν τοὺς τῆς Ἑλλάδος ἐλευθέρους πολίτας.
5. δηλώσετε τὴν τῶν πατέρων ἀρετήν.
6. ἀεὶ τιμήσεις τὸν τῶν Περσῶν βασιλέα.
7. οἱ παῖδες ἀεὶ τιμήσουσι τὰς μητέρας.
8. οἱ ἄνδρες ἐπίστευσαν τοῖς τῶν γυναικῶν ἡδέσι λόγοις.
9. ἡ μέλαινα ναῦς λυθήσεται ὑπὸ τῶν ἀνδρείων ναυτῶν.
10. ἡ τοῦ Πέρσου γυνὴ ἐπιστολὴν ἔγραψε πρὸς τὸν στρατηγόν.

XXIV. (Ex. 70-71).

1. ἐπείσαμεν τοὺς γέροντας λύσασθαι τοὺς παῖδας.
2. κελεύσομεν τοὺς στρατιώτας παύσασθαι τῆς μάχης.
3. καλὸν ἔσται λελυκέναι τὴν Ἑλλάδα.
4. ἐκελεύσαμεν τοὺς ταμίας πράττειν τὰ τῶν οἰκιῶν.
5. ἡ ἀρετὴ δηλωθήσεται ὑπὸ τῶν δούλων.
6. πάλαι ἐφιλούμεθα ὑπὸ τῶν πολιτῶν.
7. οὐ καλὸν ἔσται ὑπὸ δούλου λυθῆναι.
8. οἱ βασιλεῖς πάλαι ἐφιλοῦντο ὑπὸ τῶν πολιτῶν.
9. ἡδὺ ἔσται θέρους πεπαῦσθαι τῶν ἔργων.
10. πείσομεν τοὺς ἡγεμόνας λύεσθαι τὸν κήρυκα.

XXV. (Ex. 73-75).

1. οἱ πιστεύοντες τοῖς νόμοις πιστεύσουσι τοῖς κριταῖς.
2. ὁ στρατηγός, πείσας τοὺς στρατιώτας, ἐπιστολὴν ἔγραψεν.
3. λύσαντες τοὺς ναύτας ἐπαύσαντο τοῦ πολέμου.
4. τιμᾷ τοὺς τὴν πατρίδα σώσαντας.
5. κωλύσαντες τὴν μάχην κήρυκα ἔπεμψαν.
6. πείσαντες τοὺς πολίτας παυσόμεθα τοῦ λόγου.
7. τιμῶμεν τοὺς τὰς μάχας κωλύοντας.
8. οἱ στρατιῶται οὐκ ἐφίλουν τοὺς τὴν νίκην κωλύσαντας.
9. οἱ ἀνδρεῖοι οὐ τιμῶσι τοὺς ἀεὶ σείοντας τὰ ὅπλα.
10. οἱ τῷ βασιλεῖ πιστεύοντες οὐκ εὖ πράξουσιν ἐν τῇ Ἑλλάδι.

XXVI. (Ex. 76-79).

1. ῥᾴδιον ἔσται τοῖς εὖ πράττουσι πείθεσθαι τῷ βασιλεῖ.

2. οἱ λυσάμενοι τοὺς ναύτας ἐφιλοῦντο ὑπὸ τῶν πολιτῶν.

3. ὁ βασιλεὺς ἐτίμα τὴν τὸν ἄνδρα λελυκυῖαν.

4. οἱ ἄνδρες τιμῶσι τὰς τὰ τῶν οἰκιῶν πραττούσας.

5. αἱ γυναῖκες ἐφίλουν τὸν τοὺς παῖδας λυσάμενον.

6. οἱ λυόμενοι τοὺς στρατιώτας ὑπὸ πάντων φιλοῦνται.

7. ὁ βασιλεὺς πιστεύσει τοῖς ὑπὲρ τῆς πατρίδος μαχομένοις.

8. τιμῶσι πάντες τοὺς ἐν τῷ πολέμῳ εὖ πεπραγότας.

9. οὐχ ἡδεῖς ἦσαν τῷ γέροντι οἱ τοῦ ταμίου λόγοι.

10. οὐκ ἀεὶ τιμᾶτε τοὺς τὴν πατρίδα σεσωκότας.

XXVII. (Ex. 79-81).

1. λυθεὶς ὑπὸ τοῦ βασιλέως νῦν τιμᾷ τοὺς Πέρσας.

2. οὐ φιλοῦμεν τοὺς κρούοντας τὰς γυναῖκας.

3. οὐ τιμῶμεν τοὺς ὑπὸ τῶν γυναικῶν κρουομένους.

4. πάντες πιστεύουσι ταῖς χαριέσσαις γυναιξίν.

5. οἱ ὑπὸ τοῦ στρατηγοῦ λυθέντες χρήσιμοι ἔσονται ἐν τῷ πολέμῳ.

6. στρατιῶται ἦσαν καὶ ναῦται ἐν τῇ νήσῳ.

7. οὐ χαρίεσσαι ἀεί εἰσιν αἱ τὰ τῶν οἰκιῶν εὖ πράττουσαι.

8. οἱ λυθέντες οὐκ ἀεὶ φιλοῦσι τοὺς λύσαντας.

9. πάντες φιλοῦμεν τὰς χαριέσσας γυναῖκας.

10. οὐ τιμήσομεν τοὺς ὑπὸ τῶν γυναικῶν σῳζομένους.

XXVIII. (Ex. 82-84).

1. λύετε τὰς ναῦς, ὦ ναῦται.
2. παῦσον τὴν μάχην, ὦ κῆρυξ.
3. κελευέτω τοὺς στρατιώτας εὖ μάχεσθαι.
4. πιστεύετε τοῖς τὴν Ἑλλάδα σῴζουσιν.
5. παυόντων τὸν τῶν νεανιῶν ἀγῶνα.
6. πεῖθε τοὺς στρατηγοὺς κήρυκα πέμπειν.
7. κωλύσατε τοὺς θηρεύοντας.
8. λυσάντων τὸν ἱππέα.
9. κέλευσον τὸν παῖδα ἐπιστολὴν γράφειν πρὸς τὸν πατέρα.
10. ὁ βασιλεὺς τὸν στρατηγὸν ἐκέλευσε πάντας τοὺς ἱππέας τάττειν.

XXIX. (Ex. 85-87).

1. λύεσθε τοὺς ἀνδρείους στρατιώτας, ὦ πολῖται.
2. λυθέντων πάντες οἱ δοῦλοι.
3. παῦσαι τοῦ ἀγῶνος, ὦ νεανία.
4. οἱ νεανίαι πειθέσθων τοῖς γέρουσιν.
5. λυέσθων αἱ τῶν δούλων πέδαι.
6. κρουέσθω τὰ ὅπλα ὑπὸ τῶν στρατιωτῶν.
7. κελεύετε τοὺς παῖδας τὴν μητέρα φιλεῖν.
8. παύσασθε τοῦ ἐργοῦ, ὦ ναῦται.
9. κωλυθήτω ὁ κακῶς τὰ τῆς πόλεως πράττων.
10. κελευόντων οἱ πολῖται τὰς ναῦς πέμπειν.

XXX. (Ex. 88-90).

1. μὴ θηρεύωμεν ἐν τῇ χώρᾳ.

2. μὴ ἀεὶ πιστεύετε τοῖς εὖ πράττουσιν.

3. πείθωμεν τοὺς τὰ τῆς πόλεως πράττοντας.

4. μὴ λύσῃς τοὺς κακοὺς στρατηγούς.

5. αἰσχρόν ἐστι τοῖς δούλοις πείθεσθαι.

6. μὴ κέλευε τοὺς παῖδας τὰ αἰσχρὰ πράττειν.

7. μὴ παύσῃς τὸν καλὸν ἀγῶνα.

8. πειθώμεθα τοῖς τοὺς παῖδας παιδεύουσιν.

9. ἐδουλοῦτε τοὺς ἐλευθέρους, ὦ πολῖται.

10. δουλούσθων αἱ τῶν Περσῶν πόλεις.

XXXI. (Ex. 91-93).

1. μὴ λύσησθε τοὺς κακοὺς στρατιώτας.

2. μαχώμεθα πάντες πρὸ τῶν τειχῶν.

3. μὴ κωλύσῃς τὸν τὴν πόλιν σῴζοντα.

4. οὐ ῥᾴδιόν ἐστι τοὺς σοφοὺς πείθειν.

5. μὴ λυσώμεθα τοὺς δούλους.

6. μὴ κωλυθῶμεν ὑπὸ τῶν ῥητόρων.

7. μὴ πέμπετε τοὺς ῥήτορας πρὸς τοὺς πολεμίους.

8. πολλοί εἰσιν οἱ ὑπὲρ τοῦ βασιλέως μαχόμενοι.

9. μὴ παυθῆτε τοῦ πολέμου.

10. λυόντων τὰς ναῦς ἐν τῷ λιμένι.

XXXII. (Ex. 94-96).

1. εἰ γὰρ οἱ θεοὶ κωλύοιεν τὰς τῶν πολεμίων ναῦς.

2. μὴ οἱ πολῖται βλάπτοιεν τὸν ῥήτορα.

3. πάντες εὖ πράττοιτε.

4. εἴθ᾽ ὁ ῥήτωρ τὸν βασιλέα πείθοι.

5. μὴ βλάπτωμεν τοὺς φιλίους.

6. εἴθε μὴ παύσειε τὸν τῶν ῥητόρων ἀγῶνα.

7. μὴ πίστευε τοῖς εὐγενέσιν.

8. εἴθε σῴζοιμι τὸν πατέρα.

9. εἰ γὰρ τοὺς ἱππέας τάττοιεν ἐν τῇ ὁδῷ.

10. γράψετε πολλὰς ἐπιστολάς.

XXXIII. (Ex. 97-99).

1. μὴ παυθεῖμεν ὑπὸ τῶν κριτῶν.

2. εἴθ᾽ οἱ ἐν τῇ πόλει ναῦται πείθοιντο τῷ στρατηγῷ.

3. εἴθε λύσαισθε πᾶσαν τὴν στρατιάν.

4. πείθεσθε τοῖς τῶν σοφῶν λόγοις.

5. μὴ κωλύοιντο οἱ τὰ τῆς πόλεως πράττοντες.

6. εἰ γὰρ οἱ ἱππῆς πέμποιντο.

7. πολλοὶ καὶ αἰσχροί εἰσιν οἱ τῶν κακῶν λόγοι.

8. μὴ τὸν ῥήτορα παύσητε τῶν λόγων.

9. πειθώμεθα τοῖς τὸν ἀγῶνα παύουσιν.

10. εἴθε σῳζοίμην ἓξ ἡμερῶν.

XXXIV. (Ex. 100-102).

1. χαλεπόν ἐστι τοὺς Ἕλληνας νικᾶν.

2. ἐτιμῶμεν ἐν τῇ Ἑλλάδι τοὺς ῥήτορας.

3. μὴ τιμᾶτε τοὺς νενικημένους.

4. οἱ Ἕλληνες ἐνίκων τοὺς Πέρσας.

5. τὰ τῶν παίδων ἔργα χαλεπώτατά ἐστιν.

6. εἴθε νικῶμεν ἐν τῇ μάχῃ.

7. νίκα τοὺς κακοὺς τῇ ἀρετῇ.

8. οἱ τὰ τῆς πόλεως πράττοντες σοφώτεροί εἰσι τῶν στρατηγῶν.

9. ὁ πόλεμος δεινότερός ἐστι τῶν πάλαι πολέμων.

10. οἱ τοὺς θεοὺς τιμήσαντες νικήσουσιν.

XXXV. Ex. (103-105).

1. οἱ ῥήτορες ἐτιμῶντο ἐν τῇ Ἑλλάδι.

2. τιμάσθων οἱ σοφοὶ ὑπὸ πάντων.

3. εἴθ᾽ ὁ Δημοσθένης τιμηθείη ὑπὸ τῶν πολιτῶν.

4. τιμηθήσει, ὦ νεανία, ὑπὸ τῶν εὐγενῶν.

5. μὴ νικώμεθα, ὦ πολῖται.

6. οἱ Πέρσαι πολλάκις νενίκηνται ὑπὸ τῶν Ἑλλήνων.

7. οἱ ἐλεύθεροι ἀνδρειότεροί εἰσι τῶν δούλων.

8. οἱ δοῦλοι δώροις ἐτιμήθησαν.

9. μὴ ἀεὶ τιμᾶτε τοὺς πλουσίους.

10. εἰ γὰρ οἱ εὐγενεῖς μὴ νικῶντο ὑπὸ τῶν πλουσίων.

XXXVI. (Ex. 106-108).

1. τὸν πόλεμον ἐποιοῦντο πρὸς τοὺς Πέρσας πᾶν τὸ θέρος.
2. εὖ ποιῶμεν τοὺς ὑπὲρ τῆς πατρίδος μαχομένους.
3. εἴθε πάντες εὖ πράττοιεν.
4. μὴ πόλεμον ποιησώμεθα πρὸς τοὺς Ἕλληνας.
5. μὴ πιστεύετε τοῖς τὰ κακὰ φιλοῦσιν.
6. οἱ εὐγενεῖς οὐκ ἐφιλοῦντο ὑπὸ τῶν πολιτῶν.
7. πάντα ποιήσομεν ὑπὲρ τῶν τὴν πόλιν εὖ ποιησάντων.
8. ὁ γέρων οὐκ ἐφιλήθη ὑπὸ τῶν παίδων.
9. αἰσχρόν ἐστι κακῶς ποιεῖν τοὺς ὑπὸ τῶν πολιτῶν τιμωμένους.
10. μὴ κακῶς ποιοιης τοὺς τὸν νομον τιμῶντας.

XXXVII. (Ex. 109-111).

1. ἡ Ἑλλὰς οὐκ ἐδουλώθη ὑπὸ τῶν Περσῶν.
2. μὴ δουλοῖσθε ὑπὸ τῶν εὐγενῶν, ὦ πολῖται.
3. μὴ δηλώσητε τὰς ἐπιστολάς.
4. ἀσφαλέστερόν ἐστι δῶρα πέμπειν πρὸς τὸν βασιλέα.
5. τὰ ἐν τῇ πόλει δένδρα μελάντερά ἐστι τῶν ἐν τῇ νήσῳ
6. δουλοῖ ὑπὸ τῶν κακῶν, ὦ παῖ.
7. πάντα δηλωθήσεται τοῖς κήρυξιν.
8. πάντα δηλούσθω τοῖς ἡγεμόσιν.
9. ἐδήλουν τὰ ἐν τῷ στρατοπέδῳ ὅπλα.
10. μὴ τιμῴη τὸν τὴν πόλιν δουλώσαντα.

XXXVIII. (Ex. 112-114).

1. τὸ στρατόπεδον εὖ ἐφυλάχθη ὑπὸ τῶν νεανιῶν.
2. οἱ τὰ ὅπλα ζητοῦντες εὖ φυλαχθήσονται.
3. οἱ γέροντες ἀνδρείως πεφυλάχασι τὸ ἄστυ καὶ τὰς ναῦς.
4. ἐζήτηκα τοὺς ἱερέας ἐν τῇ πόλει.
5. σεσώκαμεν πάντα τὰ δένδρα.
6. οἱ σωφρονέστεροι πεφεύγασιν ἐν ταῖς ναυσίν.
7. πάντες οἱ τεθυκότες φεύξονται.
8. πάντα πέπρακται καὶ πάντες οἱ στρατηγοὶ πεφυλαγμένοι εἰσὶν ἐν τῷ ἄστει.
9. ἐκελεύσαμεν τοὺς ὑπὸ τῶν στρατιωτῶν φυλαττομένους φυγεῖν ἐκ τοῦ στρατοπέδου.
10. εἰ γὰρ οἱ δοῦλοι φύγοιεν.

XXXIX. (Ex. 115-117).

1. ἐψεύσθην ὑπὸ τῶν τὰ τῆς πόλεως πραττόντων.
2. εἴθ᾽ ὁ στρατηγὸς πεισθείη τὸ ἄστυ φυλάξαι.
3. οἱ στρατιῶται ἠπόρουν καὶ οὐκ ἤθελον ζητεῖν τὸν ποταμόν.
4. ἡ στρατιὰ τέτακται ἐν τῇ ὁδῷ καὶ μεγίστη ἐστίν.
5. ἡ πόλις πεφύλακται καὶ πάντες σεσωσμένοι εἰσίν.
6. τάξωμεν τὴν μείζω στρατιὰν ἐν τῇ ὁδῷ.
7. οἱ ἐψευσμένοι οὐ σωθήσονται.
8. οἱ ὑπὸ τοῦ στρατηγοῦ ταχθέντες ἤθελον ἀνδρείως μάχεσθαι.
9. πάντες πεπεισμένοι ἦσαν τὰ τείχη φυλάττειν.
10. ὁ βασιλεὺς ἔπεμψε τὰ μείζω δῶρα.

XL. (Ex. 118-120).

1. πολλοὶ ἔφυγον καὶ πλείους ἐλείφθησαν ἐν τῷ ἄστει.
2. ἐλίπομεν τοὺς παῖδας ἐν τῇ οἰκίᾳ.
3. ὁ κῆρυξ πέπεμπται πρὸς τὸν βασιλέα.
4. πέμψωμεν τοὺς φύλακας πρὸς τὸν λιμενα.
5. οἱ ὑπὸ τοῦ στρατηγοῦ πεπεμμένοι ἐν τῇ πόλει εἰσίν.
6. ᾐτήσαμεν πολλὰ δῶρα καὶ οἱ ἱερῆς πλείω αἰτοῦσιν.
7. λελείμμεθα ὀκτὼ ἔτη ἐν τῇ νήσῳ.
8. μὴ λίπητε τὰς ναῦς ἐν τῇ θαλάττῃ.
9. πλεῖστά ἐστι τὰ τοῦ βασιλέως δῶρα.
10. αἱ ἐπιστολαὶ ὑπὸ τοῦ κήρυκος γεγραμμέναι ἦσαν.

XLI. (Ex. 121-123).

1. πάντα ἤγγελται τοῖς Ἀθηναίοις.
2. ἔπειθον τοὺς πολίτας πέμπειν τὴν στρατιὰν πρὸς τὰ ὄρη.
3. οἱ πεμφθέντες πάντα ἀγγελοῦσιν.
4. πολλαὶ νῆες ἐστάλησαν ὑπὸ τῶν Ἀθηναίων.
5. οἱ πλεῖστα ἔχοντες οὐκ ἀεὶ νικήσουσιν.
6. τὰ κάλλιστα δῶρα οὐ πείσει τὸν βασιλέα.
7. οἱ εὐγενεῖς εἶχον στρατιὰν εὖ ἐσταλμένην.
8. ἐκελεύσαμεν τὸν κήρυκα πάντα ἀγγεῖλαι.
9. ἡ ἐπιστολὴ ἐγράφη ὑπὸ τῶν τὴν πόλιν εὖ ποιησάντων.
10. οἱ καλλίους ἵπποι οὐκ ἀεί εἰσι χρησιμώτεροι.

XLII. (Ex. 124-126).

1. προσέβάλομεν τοῖς τῶν πολεμίων ἱππεῦσιν.
2. συνέγραφε τὰ τῶν Ἀθηναίων.
3. οἱ τὴν πόλιν φυλάττοντες οὐκ ἐκφεύξονται.
4. ἡ θάλαττα ἔβλαψε τὰς ναῦς.
5. οἱ ἱερῆς ἐξέφευγον ἐκ τῆς χώρας.
6. πείθωμεν τὸν στρατηγὸν προσβαλεῖν τοῖς τείχεσιν.
7. πάντα ποιήσομεν τὸν ἡγεμόνα ζητοῦντες
8. ζητήσαντες τὸν ἡγεμόνα πᾶσαν τὴν ἡμέραν ἠποροῦμεν.
9. πολλοὶ συγγεγράφασι τὰ τοῦ μεγάλου πολεμου.
10. πολλὰ βέλη ἐβάλλετο εἰς τὸ στρατόπεδον.

XLIII. (Ex. 127-129)

1. ὁ λιμὴν πολὺ ἀπεῖχεν.
2. εἴθε μὴ ὁ βασιλεὺς τοὺς φύλακας καταλίποι.
3. ἀπέπεμψαν ταχέως τὸν κήρυκα πρὸς τοὺς πολεμίους.
4. ἀνδρειότατα προσβάλωμεν τῷ ἐν τοῖς ὄρεσι στρατοπέδῳ.
5. οἱ τοῖς ῥήτορσι πιστεύοντες σωφρονέστερον πάντα πράξουσιν.
6. ἡ μάχη τάχιστα ἠγγέλθη ἐν τῇ πόλει.
7. οἱ ἐν τῇ νηΐ καταλειφθέντες σοφώτερον ἔπραξαν.
8. ἀσφαλέστερόν ἐστιν ἐκ τοῦ ἄστεως ἐκφυγεῖν καὶ τον λιμένα φυλάττειν.
9. μὴ ἀεὶ ἀγγέλλετε τὰ κακά.
10. τὸ ἔργον οὐ χαλεπόν ἐστι καὶ ῥᾳδίως ὑπὸ τῶν εὐφρόνων πραχθήσεται.

XLIV. (Ex. 130-132).

1. ζητήσομεν τὰ δῶρα ἐν τῷ νεῷ.
2. οἱ πλούσιοι οὐκ ἤθελον νόμους τιθέναι ὑπὲρ τῶν πολλῶν.
3. ἔθηκαν πάντα τὰ δῶρα ἐν τῇ καλλίστῃ νηί.
4. οἱ μεθ᾽ ἡμῶν ὄντες οὐ βλάψουσι τὴν χώραν.
5. νόμους τιθῶμεν σοφώτατα καὶ σωφρονέστατα.
6. θέντες τὰ δῶρα ἐν τῷ νεῷ καὶ πάντα καταλιπόντες πρὸς ἡμᾶς ἐξέφυγον.
7. τὸ ἔργον ὑπ᾽ ἐμοῦ πέπρακται.
8. ἐτίθει τὰ ὅπλα ἐν τῇ οἰκίᾳ.
9. εἴθ᾽ οἱ σοφώτατοι τοὺς νόμους τιθεῖεν.
10. πέμψον τὸν ἀδελφὸν πρὸς ἐμὲ καὶ μὴ ἐπιστολὴν γράψῃς.

XLV. (Ex. 133-135).

1. μὴ ἐπιθώμεθα τοῖς μετὰ Δημοσθένους οὖσιν.
2. οἱ δοῦλοι ἐπέθεντο τοῖς ἐλευθέροις.
3. οἱ νικῶντες νόμους θήσουσι τοῖς νενικημένοις.
4. οἱ ναῦται οὐχ ὑμῖν ἐπιθήσονται.
5. οἱ νόμοι ἐτέθησαν ὑπὲρ τῶν πολλῶν.
6. τιθέσθω τὰ ὅπλα ἐν τῇ οἰκίᾳ.
7. μὴ βλάπτε τοὺς σοὶ πιστεύοντας.
8. οἱ ὑπὸ σοῦ πεμφθέντες μεθ᾽ ἡμῶν εἰσιν.
9. ἀνδρείως ἐπιτίθενται τῷ στρατοπέδῳ.
10. εἴθ᾽ οἱ τῆς πόλεως νόμοι ὑπὸ τῶν σοφῶν τιθεῖντο.

XLVI. Ex. (136-138).

1. ἐκελεύσαμεν αὐτοὺς τροπαῖον στῆσαι ἐν τῇ νήσῳ.
2. οἱ ναῦται ἑστήκασιν ἐν τῷ εὐρεῖ ποταμῷ.
3. οἱ κήρυκες ἔστησαν πρὸ τῶν τειχῶν.
4. καὶ οἱ νικῶντες καὶ οἱ νενικημένοι τροπαῖα ἵστασαν.
5. στῆθι μετ' ἐμοῦ ἐν ταῖς πύλαις.
6. οἱ νικῶντες τροπαῖον ἱστάντων τῆς ἐν τοῖς τείχεσι μάχης.
7. μὴ στήσωμεν τροπαῖον.
8. μὴ στῇς μετ' αὐτῶν ἐν τῇ ὁδῷ.
9. οἱ πολέμιοι αὐτὸν ἀπέπεμψαν πρὸς τὸ στρατόπεδον.
10. οἱ ἐκ τῆς μάχης πεφευγότες οὐ τροπαῖα ἱστᾶσιν.

XLVII. (Ex. 139-141).

1. ἡ ἐμὴ ἐπιστολὴ ἐγράφη ὑπὸ τοῦ ἐμοῦ ἀδελφοῦ.
2. οἱ ἐν τῇ νήσῳ ὄντες ἀφίσταντο ἀπὸ τῶν Ἀθηναίων.
3. μὴ ἀποστῶμεν ἀπὸ τῶν ἡμᾶς εὖ ποιούντων.
4. οἱ ἐν τῷ πολέμῳ ἀποστάντες οὐκ εὖ ἔπραξαν.
5. τὸ τροπαῖον ἐστάθη ὑπὸ τῶν ὑμᾶς νικησάντων.
6. οἱ Πέρσαι ἐκέλευσαν αὐτοὺς τροπαῖα ἱστάναι.
7. οἱ ἐν τῇ ὁδῷ ἑστηκότες κήρυκές εἰσιν.
8. τὰ ἐμὰ δῶρα καλλίω ἐστὶ τῶν ὑπὸ σοῦ πεμφθέντων.
9. οἱ πολλοὶ εὖ ἔπραττον καὶ οὐκ ἤθελον ἀποστῆναι.
10. αἱ γυναῖκες ἀγγελοῦσι τὴν τῶν Ἀθηναίων νίκην.

XLVIII. (Ex. 142-144).

1. τὰ μείζω δῶρα τοῖς πλουσίοις δίδομεν.
2. ἐδίδοσαν τὰ ὅπλα τοῖς στρατιώταις.
3. οἱ θεοὶ ἡμῖν διδοῖεν τὴν ἀρετήν.
4. δεδώκαμεν σοὶ τὸ μέγιστον ἔργον.
5. οἱ πολῖται τὴν οἰκίαν ἔδωκαν τῷ Δημοσθένει.
6. μὴ δίδου τοῖς εὖ πράττουσιν.
7. αἱ νῆες χρησιμώτεραι ἡμῖν εἰσι τῶν στρατιωτῶν.
8. οἱ σοὶ λόγοι ἀληθέστεροί εἰσι τῶν ἐμῶν.
9. οἱ Ἀθηναῖοι πάντα ἤθελον διδόναι τοῖς ποιηταῖς.
10. ὁ πᾶσι διδοὺς ὑπὸ πάντων φιλεῖται.

XLIX. (Ex. 145-147).

1. τὸ ἡμέτερον ἄστυ προὐδόθη ὑπὸ τῶν φυλάκων.
2. μὴ προδῶμεν τοὺς πάλαι ἡμᾶς εὖ ποιήσαντας.
3. τὰ τοῖς πλουσίοις διδόμενα οὐ χρήσιμά ἐστιν.
4. οἱ τὴν ἡμετέραν πατρίδα προδεδωκότες πρὸς ὑμᾶς φεύγουσιν.
5. ὁ ἵππος ἐδόθη τῷ ἀνδρειοτάτῳ στρατιώτῃ.
6. τὰ κάλλιστα δῶρα τοῖς πλουσίοις δίδοται.
7. αἱ ἡμέτεραι πόλεις προδοθήσονται τοῖς πολεμίοις.
8. τοῦ χειμῶνος πολλαὶ πόλεις ἀποστήσονται.
9. εἴθε μὴ οἱ νεῲ προδοθεῖεν.
10. διδῶμεν τὰ ὅπλα τοῖς ἐν τῷ τείχει ἑστηκόσιν.

L. (Ex. 148-150).

1. ἴωμεν πρὸς τοὺς πολεμίους.
2. ἐλθόντες πρὸς ἡμᾶς ἐν τῇ ἡμετέρᾳ οἰκίᾳ ἦσαν
3. ᾔει μετὰ τῶν ἀδελφῶν.
4. ἴτε, ὦ νεανίαι, πρὸς τὴν ὑμετέραν πόλιν.
5. τῇ ἐνάτῃ ἡμέρᾳ ἡ ναῦς ἔσται ἐν τῷ λιμένι.
6. ἐδείκνυσαν τοὺς καλλίστους νεώς.
7. μετὰ τὴν μάχην ὁ Δημοσθένης στρατηγὸς ἀπεδείχθη.
8. εἴθ' οἱ παῖδες ἀσφαλῶς ἔλθοιεν.
9. ὁ ἐμὸς ἀδελφὸς εἰσι πρὸς τὴν πόλιν καὶ τὸν κριτὴν ζητήσει.
10. ἴσθι ἀνδρεῖος, ὦ νεανία, καὶ φύλαττε τοὺς σοὶ πισ· τεύοντας.

LI. (Ex. 151-153).

1. οὗτοι τὴν νίκην ἠγγέλκασιν.
2. αὗται αἱ νῆες τοῖς πολίταις ἐδόθησαν ὑπὸ τοῦ Δημοσ· θένους.
3. ταῦτα τὰ δένδρα ἐθαυμάσθη ὑπὸ τῶν Περσῶν.
4. οἱ θεοὶ αὐξάνοιεν τὴν τῶν πολιτῶν ἀρετήν.
5. ἡ τῶν στρατιωτῶν ἐλπὶς ηὐξήθη ταύτῃ τῇ νίκῃ.
6. οἱ ἐν τοῖς ὄρεσι μαχεσάμενοι νυκτὸς ἦσαν πρὸς τὴν πόλιν.
7. ἐθαυμάσαμεν τὰ τούτων τῶν γυναικῶν δῶρα.
8. ἐκέλευσαν τοὺς κήρυκας πρὸς τὸ στρατόπεδον ἐλθόντας πάντα τοῖς ἀποστᾶσιν ἀγγεῖλαι.
9. ἡ ταύτης τῆς γυναικὸς ἀρετὴ μείζων ἐστὶ τῆς τῶν ἀνδρῶν.
10. μὴ θαυμάζετε τοὺς τὴν πατρίδα βλάπτοντας.

LII. (Ex. 154-156).

1. μείνωμεν ἐν ἐκείνῃ τῇ οἰκίᾳ.

2. πολλὰ δῶρα ἐδέξαντο ἐν τῇ πόλει μένοντες.

3. εἰπὲ τοῦτο τοῖς ὑπὸ τοῦ στρατηγοῦ πεμφθεῖσιν.

4. οὐκ ἐροῦμεν τοῦτο τοῖς κριταῖς.

5. ἐκέλευσαν τὴν στρατιὰν πορευθῆναι τῇ ἕκτῃ ἡμέρᾳ.

6. οἱ ναῦται ἔμενον ἐν ταῖς ναυσίν.

7. τὸ στρατόπεδόν ἐστιν ἐν ἐκείνοις τοῖς ὄρεσιν.

8. ἐκεῖνο τὸ δένδρον κάλλιον ἐστι τούτου.

9. μενοῦμεν ἐν τῇ ὁδῷ ἑστηκότες.

10. ἐπορευόμεθα τρεῖς ἡμέρας ἐν ἐκείνῃ τῇ χώρᾳ.

LIII. (Ex. 157-159).

1. οἱ πολῖται αὐτοὶ οὐκ ἐβούλοντο ἀποστῆναι.

2. ἀποθανεῖ ὑπ' αὐτῶν τῶν φιλῶν.

3. οὐκ ἤθελεν ἡγεμὼν γενέσθαι.

4. οὐκ ἀποκτείναντες τὸν βασιλέα αὐτοὶ ἀπέθανον.

5. ἡ γυνὴ αὐτὴ ἀπέκτεινε τὸν ἄνδρα.

6. μὴ ἀποκτείνωμεν τοὺς πρὸς ἡμᾶς πεφευγότας.

7. τοῦτο ποιήσας βασιλεὺς γενήσει τῆς πάσης χώρας.

8. ἡγεμὼν γενοῦ τῶν ἀποστάντων καὶ νικήσεις.

9. φύλακας δεξάμενος τοὺς πολίτας κακῶς ἐποίει.

10. τοῦτ' εἰπὼν ἐβουλήθη πρὸς τὸν λιμένα ἰέναι.

LIV. (Ex. 160-162).

1. πορευθέντες χαλεπωτάτῃ ὁδῷ εἰς τὸ στρατόπεδον ἀφίκοντο.

2. ὁ κῆρυξ ἀφῖκται καὶ αὐτὸς ταῦτα ἀγγελεῖ.

3. μὴ διαφθείρωμεν τὰ τῶν φιλίων.

4. ταῦτα τείχη φυλάττει καὶ τὴν πόλιν καὶ τὸν λιμένα.

5. ἀσφαλέστερον ἔσται τὴν οἰκίαν αὐτὴν διαφθεῖραι.

6. οὐ σώσομεν τὰ ὑπὸ τῶν πολεμίων διαφθαρέντα.

7. ἡ πόλις διέφθαρται καὶ πάντες οἱ ἐν αὐτῇ τεθνήκασιν.

8. οἱ ἄνδρες καὶ αἱ γυναῖκες εἶχον τὴν αὐτὴν ἀρετήν.

9. εἴθ᾽ αἱ νῆες εἰς τὸν λιμένα ἀφίκοιντο.

10. αὐτοὶ πολῖται πάλαι ἔσωσαν καὶ νῦν διαφθείρουσι τὴν πόλιν.

LV. (Ex. 163-165).

1. εἶδον τοὺς ὑπὸ τῶν ἱππέων ληφθέντας.

2. ἰδόντες τοὺς φύλακας οὐκ ἐμείναμεν.

3. μὴ λάβωμεν τὰ τῶν κακῶν δῶρα.

4. ἡ ἡμετέρα πόλις πολλάκις εἴληπται ὑπὸ τῶν αὐτῶν πολεμίων.

5. εἴθε μὴ ταῦτα ὁρῷμεν.

6. λαβόντες τὰς πόλεις πάντα τὰ ἐν αὐταῖς ὄντα διαφθεροῦμεν.

7. αἱ ταχεῖαι νῆες οὐ ληφθήσονται.

8. αὐτὸς ἑόρακα δεινότερα ἐν τοῖς πάλαι πολέμοις.

9. ἀφικόμενοι ταχέως εἰς τὸν νεὼν ἀποκτείνατε τὸν ἱερέα.

10. στρατηγὸς γενόμενος αὐτὸς τοὺς στρατιώτας κακῶς ἐποίει.

SPECIAL VOCABULARIES

N.B.—In the following Vocabularies genders are given (except where the meaning makes it unnecessary) and the genitives of all nouns.

Exercises 1-3.

I loose, loosen, free, set free, λύω
sea, θάλαττα, -ης, *f.*
Muse, μοῦσα, -ης, *f.*
tongue, γλῶττα, -ης, *f.*
country, χώρα, -ας, *f.*
battle, μάχη, -ης, *f.*
virtue, courage, valour, bravery, ἀρετή, -ῆς, *f.*
I stop (*transitive*), παύω
wisdom, σοφία, -ας, *f.*
in, ἐν (*dative*)
goddess, θεά, -ᾶς
fetters, πέδαι, -ῶν, *f. pl.*

Exercises 4-6.

house, οἰκία, -ας, *f.*
army, στρατιά, -ᾶς, *f.*
honour, τιμή, -ῆς, *f.*
victory, νίκη, -ης, *f.*
land, earth, γῆ, -ῆς, *f.*
I prevent, κωλύω
I hunt, pursue, θηρεύω
and, καί

Exercises 7-9.

young man, νεανίας, -ου
steward, ταμίας, -ου
citizen, πολίτης, -ου
judge, κριτής, -οῦ

from, out of, ἐκ (*genitive*): *before vowels* ἐξ
I train, παιδεύω

Exercises 10-12.

sailor, ναύτης, -ου
soldier, στρατιώτης, -ου
gate, πύλη, -ης, *f.*
to (*meaning 'motion to'*), πρός (*accusative*)
into, εἰς (*accusative*)

Exercises 13-15.

word, λόγος, -ου, *m.*
man (= Latin *homo*), ἄνθρωπος, -ου
war, πόλεμος, -ου, *m.*
river, ποταμός, -οῦ, *m.*
general, στρατηγός, -οῦ
law, νόμος, -ου, *m.*
not, οὐ (οὐκ before vowel with soft breathing, οὐχ before vowel with rough breathing)
O, ὦ (with *vocative*)

Exercises 16-18.

deed, task, work, ἔργον, -ου, *n.*
camp, στρατόπεδον, -ου, *n.*
gift, present, δῶρον, -ου, *n.*
tree, δένδρον, -ου, *n.* (*irreg. dat. pl.* δένδρεσι(ν))

141

arm, weapon, ὅπλον, -ov, n.
horse, ἵππος, -ov, m.
yoke, ζυγόν, -οῦ, n.
slave, δοῦλος, -ov, m.
head, κεφαλή, -ῆς, f.
is, ἐστί(ν)
are, εἰσί(ν)
I shake, brandish, σείω
I strike, κρούω

Exercises 19-21.

island, νῆσος, -ov, f.
road, ὁδός, -οῦ, f.
wise, clever, σοφός, -ή, -όν
good, ἀγαθός, -ή, -όν
friendly, φίλιος, -α, -ον
trust, believe, πιστεύω (dative)

Exercises 22-24.

poet, ποιητής, -οῦ, m.
brother, ἀδελφός, -οῦ
useful, χρήσιμος, -η, -ον
free, ἐλεύθερος, -α, -ον
often, πολλάκις

Exercises 25-27.

brave, ἀνδρεῖος, -α, -ον
difficult,
troublesome, } χαλεπός, -ή, -όν
beautiful,
honourable, } καλός, -ή, -όν
disgraceful, base,
ugly, } αἰσχρός, -ά, -όν
I order, κελεύω

Exercises 31-33.

guard, φύλαξ, gen. φύλακος, m.
herald, κῆρυξ, gen. κήρυκος, m.

do, transact,
fare, { πράττω,   πράξω,
ἔπραξα, πέπραχα.
(When = ' fare ' the
perf. is πέπραγα)

well, εὖ
badly, κακῶς
draw up, τάττω, τάξω, ἔταξα,
τέταχα
the affairs of . . ., use τά with
gen. sing. (= the things of . . .),
e.g. the affairs of the general,
τὰ τοῦ στρατηγοῦ

Exercises 34-36.

send, πέμπω, πέμψω, ἔπεμψα, πέ-
πομφα
terrible, δεινός, -ή, -όν

Exercises 37-39.

country (= native country), πατρίς,
gen. πατρίδος, f.
Greece, Ἑλλάς, gen. Ἑλλάδος, f.
affair, πρᾶγμα, gen. πράγματος, n.
body, σῶμα, gen. σώματος, n.
old man, γέρων, gen. γέροντος, m.
lion, λέων, gen. λέοντος, m.
I persuade, πείθω, πείσω, ἔπεισα,
πέπεικα
save, keep, preserve, σῴζω, σώσω,
ἔσωσα, σέσωκα
then (= at that time), τότε
now, νῦν
boy, child, son, παῖς, gen. παιδός, c.

Exercises 40-42.

day, ἡμέρα, -ας, f.
night, νύξ, gen. νυκτός, f.
month, μήν, gen. μηνός, m.
Greek, Ἕλλην, gen. Ἕλληνος, m.

leader, ἡγεμών, gen. ἡγεμόνος, m.
contest, ἀγών, gen. ἀγῶνος, m.
letter, ἐπιστολή, -ῆς, f.
I write, γράφω, γράψω, ἔγραψα, γέγραφα, aor. pass. ἐγράφην

Exercises 43-45.

I ransom, λύομαι (middle)
Demosthenes, Δημοσθένης, gen. Δημοσθένους
Socrates, Σωκράτης, gen. Σωκράτους
kind, kindly, εὔφρων, -ον
noble, εὐγενής, -ές
the nobles, οἱ εὐγενεῖς
true, ἀληθής, -ές

Exercises 46-48.

I cease, παύομαι (middle)
I cease from, παύομαι with genitive case
race, γένος, gen. γένους, n.
year, ἔτος, gen. ἔτους, n.
summer, θέρος, gen. θέρους, n.

Exercises 49-51.

city, state, πόλις, gen. πόλεως, f.
power, δύναμις, gen. δυνάμεως, f.

Exercises 52-54.

fish, ἰχθύς, gen. ἰχθύος, m.
city, ἄστυ, gen. ἄστεως, n.
sweet, pleasant, pleasing, ἡδύς, ἡδεῖα, ἡδύ
short, βραχύς, βραχεῖα, βραχύ
broad, εὐρύς, εὐρεῖα, εὐρύ
by (=personal agency), ὑπό, (genitive)

Exercises 55-57.

king, βασιλεύς, gen. βασιλέως
horseman, ἱππεύς, gen. ἱππέως
cavalry, ἱππῆς (pl.)
Persian, Πέρσης, -ου
always, ἀεί

Exercises 58-60.

orator, rhetorician, ῥήτωρ, gen. ῥήτορος, m.
I honour, τιμῶ (-άω)
god, θεός, -οῦ, m.

Exercises 61-63.

father, πατήρ, gen. πατρός
mother, μητήρ, gen. μητρός
I do, make, ποιῶ (-έω)
I love, φιλῶ (-έω)
I treat well, εὖ ποιῶ
I treat badly, ill, κακῶς ποιῶ

Exercises 64-66.

man (=Latin vir), husband, ἀνήρ, gen. ἀνδρός
I show, δηλῶ (-όω)
I enslave, δουλῶ (-όω)
bad, wicked, κακός, κακή, κακόν

Exercises 67-69.

woman, wife, γυνή, gen. γυναικός
ship, ναῦς, gen. νεώς, f.
black, μέλας, μέλαινα, μέλαν

Exercises 70-72.

easy, ῥᾴδιος, ῥᾳδία, ῥᾴδιον
easily, ῥᾳδίως
formerly, πάλαι
labour, ἔργον
manage, πράττω

Exercises 73-75.

all, πᾶς, πᾶσα, πᾶν
speech, λόγος
I prosper, εὖ πράττω
the prosperous, οἱ εὖ πράττοντες

Exercises 76-78.

I fight, μάχομαι
I obey, πείθομαι (dative)
I serve, benefit, εὖ ποιῶ (εω)
for (=on behalf of), ὑπέρ (genitive)

Exercises 79-81.

harbour, λιμήν, gen. λιμένος, m.
graceful, χαρίεις, χαρίεσσα, χαρίεν

Exercises 82-84.

much, many, πολύς, πολλή, πολύ
the many, οἱ πολλοί

Exercises 85-87.

great, large, big, μέγας, μεγάλη, μέγα

Exercises 88-90.

tooth, ὀδούς, gen. ὀδόντος, m.
sharp, ὀξύς, ὀξεῖα, ὀξύ
kind (noun), γένος, gen. γένους, n.
accomplish, πράττω

Exercises 91-93.

wall, τεῖχος, gen. τείχους, n.
in front of, πρό (genitive)
enemy, πολέμιος, -ου, m.

Exercises 94-96.

Oh that (=a wish), use the optative mood
I harm, βλάπτω, βλάψω, ἔβλαψα, βέβλαφα
god, θεός, -οῦ, m.

Exercises 97-99.

every, πᾶς, πᾶσα, πᾶν (without article)
the whole, πᾶς (with the article)
I administer, πράττω

Exercises 100-102.

I conquer, defeat, νικῶ (-αω), νικήσω, ἐνίκησα, νενίκηκα
the conquerors, οἱ νενικηκότες
the conquered, οἱ νενικημένοι

Exercises 103-105.

rich, πλούσιος, -α, -ον

Exercises 106-108.

I carry on the war against, τὸν πόλεμον ποιοῦμαι πρός (accusative)
winter, χειμών, gen. χειμῶνος, m.
benefactors, οἱ εὖ ποιοῦντες

Exercises 109-111.

safe, ἀσφαλής, -ές
spring, ἔαρ, gen. ἦρος, n.

Exercises 112-114.

temperate, σώφρων, -ον
fly, flee from, avoid, φεύγω, φεύξομαι, ἔφυγον, πέφευγα
I accomplish, πράττω, aor. pass. ἐπράχθην, perf. pass. πέπραγμαι

everything, πάντα (neuter plural)
priest, ἱερεύς, gen. ἱερέως, m.
I sacrifice, θύω, θύσω, ἔθυσα,
τέθυκα
I guard, φυλάττω, φυλάξω, ἐφύλαξα,
πεφύλαχα, ἐφυλάχθην, πεφύ-
λαγμαι
I seek, ζητῶ (εω), ζητήσω, ἐζήτησα,
ἐζήτηκα

Exercises 115-117.

I deceive, ψεύδω, ψεύσω, ἔψευσα,
ἐψεύσθην, ἔψευσμαι
I lie, tell lies, ψεύδομαι
I am perplexed, ἀπορῶ (εω), (impf.
ἠπόρουν), ἀπορήσω, ἠπόρησα
I am willing, ἐθέλω, (impf. ἤθελον),
ἐθελήσω, ἠθέλησα, ἠθέληκα
I would not obey (=I was unwill-
ing to), οὐκ ἤθελον πείθεσθαι
I save, σῴζω, aor. pass. ἐσώθην
I draw up, τάττω, aor. pass.
ἐτάχθην, perf. pass. τέταγμαι

Exercises 118-120.

I leave, forsake, λείπω, λείψω,
ἔλιπον, λέλοιπα, ἐλείφθην,
λέλειμμαι
fellow-citizen, πολίτης, -ου, m.
I ask for, αἰτῶ (εω), (impf. ᾔτουν),
αἰτήσω, ᾔτησα, ᾔτηκα
rank, τάξις, gen. τάξεως, f.
I send, πέμπω, aor. pass. ἐπέμφθην
perf. pass. πέπεμμαι

Exercises 121-123.

I equip, fit out, στέλλω, στελῶ,
ἔστειλα, ἔσταλκα, ἐστάλην,
ἔσταλμαι
Athenian, Ἀθηναῖος, -ου

I advise, πείθω
mountain, ὄρος, gen. ὄρους, n.
I announce, report, ἀγγέλλω,
ἀγγελῶ, ἤγγειλα, ἤγγελκα,
ἠγγέλθην, ἤγγελμαι
I have, possess, ἔχω (impf. εἶχον),
ἕξω

Exercises 124-126.

missile, dart, βέλος, gen. βέλους, n.
I throw, βάλλω, ἔβαλλον, βαλῶ,
ἔβαλον, βέβληκα
I attack, προσβάλλω, προσέβαλ-
λον, προσβαλῶ, προσέβαλον
(dative)
I escape, ἐκφεύγω, ἐξέφευγον,
ἐκφεύξομαι, ἐξέφυγον
I write a history, συγγράφω,
συνέγραφον, συγγράψω, συνέ-
γραψα, συγγέγραφα
I wrote a history of Greece, συνέ-
γραψα τὰ τῆς Ἑλλάδος

Exercises 127-129.

bravely, ἀνδρείως
wisely, σοφῶς
temperately, σωφρόνως
quickly, ταχέως
I act, πράττω
much (adv.), far, πολύ
I am distant, ἀπέχω, impf.
ἀπεῖχον
I leave behind, καταλείπω, κατέ-
λειπον, καταλείψω, κατέλιπον
I send away, despatch, ἀποπέμπω,
ἀπέπεμπον, ἀποπέμψω, ἀπέπεμψα
from, ἀπό (genitive)

Exercises 130-132.

I place, put, τίθημι, ἐτίθην, θήσω
ἔθηκα, τέθηκα

I enact a law, νόμον τίθημι

I, ἐγώ

temple, νεώς, gen. νεώ, m.

hope, ἐλπίς, -ίδος, f.

with, together with (= Latin cum), μετά (genitive)

Exercises 133-135.

thou, σύ

I attack, ἐπιτίθεμαι, ἐπετιθέμην, ἐπιθήσομαι, ἐπεθέμην (dative)

young, νέος, νέα, νέον.

Exercises 136-138.

I set up, ἵστημι, ἵστην, στήσω, ἔστησα

I stan'd, ἔστηκα

I stood, ἔστην

him, αὐτόν

trophy, τροπαῖον, -ου, n.

both . . . and . . . καί . . . καί . . .

Exercises 139-141.

I revolt, ἀφίσταμαι, ἀφιστάμην, ἀποστήσομαι, ἀπέστην, ἀφέστηκα

my, ἐμός

Exercises 142-144.

I give, δίδωμι, ἐδίδουν, δώσω, ἔδωκα, δέδωκα, ἐδόθην

your (= Latin tuus), σός, σή, σόν

Exercises 145-147.

I betray, προδίδωμι, προὐδίδουν, προδώσω, προὔδωκα, προδέδωκα, προὐδόθην

our, ἡμέτερος, -α, -ον

Exercises 148-150.

I show, δείκνυμι, ἐδείκνυν, δείξω, ἔδειξα, ἐδείχθην

I display, appoint, ἀποδείκνυμι, ἀπεδείκνυν, ἀποδείξω, ἀπέδειξα, ἀπεδείχθην

after, μετά (accusative)

your (= Latin vester), ὑμέτερος, -α, -ον

I go, come, ἔρχομαι, ᾖα, εἶμι, ἦλθον, ἐλήλυθα

Exercises 151-153.

this, οὗτος, αὕτη, τοῦτο

I admire, wonder at, θαυμάζω, ἐθαύμαζον, θαυμάσομαι, ἐθαύμασα, τεθαύμακα, ἐθαυμάσθην

I fight, μάχομαι, ἐμαχόμην, μαχοῦμαι, ἐμαχεσάμην, μεμάχημαι

I increase (transitive), αὐξάνω, ηὔξανον, αὐξήσω, ηὔξησα, ηὔξηκα, ηὐξήθην

Exercises 154-156.

that (= Latin ille), ἐκεῖνος, -η, -ο

I remain, await, stay, μένω, ἔμενον, μενῶ, ἔμεινα, μεμένηκα

I receive, δέχομαι, ἐδεχόμην, δέξομαι, ἐδεξάμην, δέδεγμαι

I say, tell, speak, λέγω, ἔλεγον, ἐρῶ, εἶπον, εἴρηκα

I march, πορεύομαι, ἐπορευόμην, πορεύσομαι, ἐπορεύθην

Exercises 157-159.

self (= Latin ipse), αὐτός, αὐτή, αὐτό

I wish, βούλομαι, ἐβουλόμην, βουλήσομαι, ἐβουλήθην

I become, γίγνομαι, ἐγιγνόμην, γενήσομαι, ἐγενόμην

I kill, ἀποκτείνω, ἀπέκτεινον, ἀποκτενῶ, ἀπέκτεινα, ἀπέκτονα

I die, am killed, ἀποθνήσκω, ἀπέθνησκον, ἀποθανοῦμαι, ἀπέθανον, τέθνηκα

Exercises 160-162.

the same, ὁ αὐτός, ἡ αὐτή, τὸ αὐτό

I destroy, corrupt, διαφθείρω, διέφθειρον, διαφθερῶ, διέφθειρα, διέφθαρκα, διεφθάρην, διέφθαρμαι

I arrive, ἀφικνοῦμαι, ἀφικνούμην, ἀφίξομαι, ἀφικόμην, ἀφῖγμαι at, in (*after* '*arrive*'), εἰς (*accusative*)

Exercises 163-165.

I see, ὁρῶ (αω), ἑώρων, ὄψομαι, εἶδον, ἑόρακα

I take, λαμβάνω, ἐλάμβανον, λήψομαι, ἔλαβον, εἴληφα, ἐλήφθην

GENERAL VOCABULARIES

ENGLISH-GREEK

accomplish, I,
act, I, } πράττω
administer, I,
admire, I, θαυμάζω
advise, I, πείθω
affair, πρᾶγμα
affairs of, the, τά, *with genitive case*
(Voc. 31)
after, μετά (*acc.*)
against (*after* 'carry on war'),
πρός (*acc.*)
all, πᾶς
always, ἀεί
am, I, εἰμί
and, καί
announce, I, ἀγγέλλω
appoint, I, ἀποδείκνυμι
are, they, εἰσί(ν)
arm, ὅπλον
army, στρατιά
arrive, I, ἀφικνοῦμαι
ask for, I, αἰτῶ (εω)
at (*after* 'arrive'), εἰς (*acc.*)
at (*after* 'wonder'), *use acc. case*
Athenian, Ἀθηναῖος
attack, I, προσβάλλω (*dat.*)
,, ἐπιτίθεμαι (*dat.*)
avoid, I, φεύγω
await, I, μένω
away, I send, ἀποπέμπω.

bad, κακός
badly, κακῶς

badly, I fare, κακῶς πράττω
badly, I treat, κακῶς ποιῶ (εω)
base, αἰσχρός
battle, μάχη
beautiful, καλός
become, I, γίγνομαι
before, πρό (*gen.*)
behalf of, on, ὑπέρ (*gen.*)
behind, I leave, καταλείπω
believe, I, πιστεύω
benefactors, οἱ εὖ ποιοῦντες
benefit, I, εὖ ποιῶ (εω)
betray, προδίδωμι
big, μέγας
black, μέλας
body, σῶμα
both . . . and, καί . . . καί
boy, παῖς
brandish, I, σείω
brave, ἀνδρεῖος
bravely, ἀνδρείως
bravery, ἀρετή
broad, εὐρύς
brother, ἀδελφός
by (instrument), *use dative case*
by (agent), ὑπό (*gen.*).

camp, στρατόπεδον
carry on the war, I, τὸν πόλεμον
ποιοῦμαι
cavalry, ἱππῆς (*pl.*)
cease, I, παύομαι
child, παῖς
citizen, πολίτης

city, πόλις, ἄστυ
clever, σοφός
come, I, ἔρχομαι (p. 100)
conquer, I, νικῶ (αω)
conquerors, the, οἱ νενικηκότες
conquered, the, οἱ νενικημένοι
contest, ἀγών
corrupt, I, διαφθείρω
country, χώρα
country, native, πατρίς
courage, ἀρετή.

dart, βέλος
day, ἡμέρα
deceive, I, ψεύδω
deed, ἔργον
defeat, I, νικῶ (αω)
Demosthenes, Δημοσθένης
despatch, I, ἀποπέμπω
destroy, I, διαφθείρω
die, I, ἀποθνῄσκω
difficult, χαλεπός
disgraceful, αἰσχρός
display, ἀποδείκνυμι
distant, I am, ἀπέχω
do, I, πράττω, ποιῶ (εω)
draw up, I, τάττω.

earth, γῆ
easily, ῥᾳδίως
easy, ῥᾴδιος
eight, ὀκτώ
eighth, ὄγδοος
eleven, ἕνδεκα
eleventh, ἑνδέκατος
equip, I, στέλλω
escape, I, ἐκφεύγω
escape from, I, ἐκφεύγω ἐκ (gen.)
enact, I, τίθημι
enemy, πολέμιος
enslave, I, δουλῶ (οω)

every, πᾶς (without article)
everything, πάντα.

far, πολύ
fare, I, πράττω
father, πατήρ
fellow-citizen, πολίτης
fetters, πέδαι
fifth, πέμπτος
fight, I, μάχομαι
first, πρῶτος
fish, ἰχθύς
fit out, I, στέλλω
five, πέντε
flee, I, φεύγω
fly, I, φεύγω
for (= on behalf of), ὑπέρ (gen.)
formerly, πάλαι
forsake, I, λείπω
four, τέτταρες
fourth, τέταρτος
free, I,   } λύω
free, I set,
free, (adj.), ἐλεύθερος
friendly, φίλιος
from, ἀπό (gen.)
  ,, (after ' escape'), ἐκ (gen.)
  ,, (after ' flee, fly '), use accusative case
front of, in, πρό (gen.).

gate, πύλη
general, στρατηγός
gift, δῶρον
give, I, δίδωμι
go, I, ἔρχομαι (p. 100)
god, θεός
goddess, θεά
good, ἀγαθός
graceful, χαρίεις
great, μέγας
Greece, Ἑλλάς

Greek, Ἕλλην
guard (noun), φύλαξ
guard, I, φυλάττω.

harbour, λιμήν
hard, χαλεπός
harm, I, βλάπτω
have, I, ἔχω
head, κεφαλή
herald, κῆρυξ
him, αὐτόν
history, I write a, συγγράφω
honour (noun), τιμή
honour, I, τιμῶ (αω)
honourable, καλός
hope, ἐλπίς
horse, ἵππος
horseman, ἱππεύς
house, οἰκία
husband, ἀνήρ
hunt, I, θηρεύω.

I, ἐγώ
ill, I treat, κακῶς ποιῶ (εω)
ill, I fare, κακῶς πράττω
in, ἐν (dat.)
,, (after ' arrive'), εἰς (acc.)
,, front of, πρό (gen.)
increase, I (trans.), αὐξάνω
into, εἰς (acc.)
is, ἐστί(ν)
island, νῆσος.

judge, κριτής.

keep, I, σῴζω, φυλάττω
kill, 1, ἀποκτείνω
killed, 1 am, ἀποθνῄσκω
kind (noun), γένος
kind (adj.) ⎫
kindly,   ⎬ εὔφρων
king, βασιλεύς.

labour, ἔργον
land, γῆ
large, μέγας
law, νόμος
leader, ἡγεμών
leave, I, λείπω
leave behind, I, καταλείπω
letter, ἐπιστολή
lie, I,   ⎫
lies, I tell, ⎬ ψεύδομαι
lion, λέων
loose, loosen, I, λύω
love, I, φιλῶ (εω)

make, I, ποιῶ (εω)
man (=homo), ἄνθρωπος
,, (=vir), ἀνήρ
,, old, γέρων
,, young, νεανίας
manage, I, πράττω
many, πολύς
many, the, οἱ πολλοί
march, I, πορεύομαι
missile, βέλος
month, μήν
mother, μήτηρ
mountain, ὄρος
much (adj.), πολύς
much (adv.), πολύ
Muse, μοῦσα
my, ἐμός.

night, νύξ
nine, ἐννέα
ninth, ἔνατος
noble, εὐγενής
not, οὐ
,, (with subjunctive, imperative,
optative), μή
now, νῦν.

O, ὦ
obey, I, πείθομαι (dat.)
of, in front, πρό (gen.)
of, out, ἐκ (gen.)
often, πολλάκις
Oh that (= a wish), use the optative
    mood
old man, γέρων
one, εἷς, μία, ἕν
orator, ῥήτωρ
order, I, κελεύω
our, ἡμέτερος
out of, ἐκ (gen.).

perplexed, I am, ἀπορῶ (εω)
Persian, Πέρσης
persuade, I, πείθω
place, I, τίθημι
pleasant, } ἡδύς
pleasing,
poet, ποιητής
possess, I, ἔχω
power, δύναμις
present, δῶρον
preserve, I, σώζω
prevent, I, κωλύω
priest, ἱερεύς
prosper, I, εὖ πράττω
prosperous, the, οἱ εὖ πράττοντες
pursue, I, θηρεύω
put, I, τίθημι.

quickly, ταχέως.

race, γένος
rank, τάξις
ransom, I, λύομαι
receive, I, δέχομαι, λαμβάνω
remain, I, μένω
report, I, ἀγγέλλω
revolt, I, ἀφίσταμαι
rhetorician, ῥήτωρ
rich, πλούσιος
river, ποταμός

road, ὁδός.
sacrifice, I, θύω
safe, ἀσφαλής
sailor, ναύτης
same, the, ὁ αὐτός
save, I, σώζω
say, I, λέγω (Voc. 154 and p. 104)
sea, θάλαττα
second, δεύτερος
see, I, ὁρῶ (αω)
seek, I, ζητῶ (εω)
self, αὐτός
send, I, πέμπω
send away, I, ἀποπέμπω
serve, I, εὖ ποιῶ (εω)
set free, I, λύω
set up, I, ἵστημι
seven, ἑπτά
seventh, ἕβδομος
shake, I, σείω
sharp, ὀξύς
ship, ναῦς
short, βραχύς
show, I, δηλῶ (οω), δείκνυμι
six, ἕξ
sixth, ἕκτος
slave, δοῦλος
Socrates, Σωκράτης
soldier, στρατιώτης
son, παῖς
speak, I, λέγω (Voc. 154 and p. 104)
speech, λόγος
spring, ἔαρ
stand, I, ἕστηκα
state, πόλις
stay, μένω
steward, ταμίας
stood, I, ἔστην
stop, I, παύω
strike, I, κρούω
summer, θέρος
sweet, ἡδύς

take, I, λαμβάνω
task, ἔργον
tell, I, λέγω (Voc. 154 and p. 104)
temperate, σώφρων
temperately, σωφρόνως
temple, νεώς
ten, δέκα
tenth, δέκατος
terrible, δεινός
that, ἐκεῖνος
the, ὁ, ἡ, τό
then, τότε
third, τρίτος
this, οὗτος
thou, σύ
three, τρεῖς
throw, I, βάλλω
to (=motion to), πρός (acc.)
together with, μετά (gen.)
tongue, γλῶττα
tooth, ὀδούς
train, I, παιδεύω
transact, I, πράττω
treat badly, ill, I, κακῶς ποιῶ
treat well, I, εὖ ποιῶ
tree, δένδρον
trophy, τροπαῖον
troublesome, χαλεπός
true, ἀληθής
trust, I, πιστεύω (dat.)
twelfth, δωδέκατος
twelve, δώδεκα
two, δύο.

ugly, αἰσχρός
useful, χρήσιμος.

valour, ἀρετή
victory, νίκη
virtue, ἀρετή.

wall, τεῖχος
war, πόλεμος
weapon, ὅπλον
well, εὖ
well, I fare, εὖ πράττω
well, I treat, εὖ ποιῶ (εω)
whole, the, πᾶς (with article)
wife, γυνή
winter, χειμών
willing, I am, ἐθέλω
wisdom, σοφία
wise, σοφός
wisely, σοφῶς
wish, I, βούλομαι
with (=instrument), use dative case
with (=together with), μετά (gen.)
woman, γυνή
wonder at, I, θαυμάζω
word, λόγος
work, ἔργον
write, I, γράφω
write a history, I, συγγράφω.

year, ἔτος
yoke, ζυγόν
young, νέος
young man, νεανίας
your (=tuus), σός
  ,, (=vester), ὑμέτερος.

GREEK-ENGLISH

ἀγαθός, good
ἀγγέλλω, I announce
ἀγών, contest
ἀδελφός, brother
ἀεί, always
'Αθηναῖος, Athenian
αἰσχρός, base, disgraceful, ugly
αἰτῶ, I ask for
ἀληθής, true
ἀνδρεῖος, brave
ἀνδρείως, bravely
ἀνήρ, man, husband
ἄνθρωπος, man
ἀπέχω, I am distant
ἀπό, from
ἀποδείκνυμι, I appoint, display
ἀποθνήσκω, I die, am killed
ἀποκτείνω, I kill
ἀποπέμπω, I send away, despatch
ἀπορῶ, I am perplexed
ἀρετή, courage, virtue
ἄστυ, city
ἀσφαλής, safe
αὐτός, self ; in oblique cases him,
    her, it, them ; preceded by article
    the same
αὐξάνω, I increase
ἀφικνοῦμαι, I arrive
ἀφίσταμαι, I revolt.

βάλλω, I throw
βασιλεύς, king
βέλος, dart, missile
βλάπτω, I harm
βούλομαι, I wish
βραχύς, short.

γένος, race, kind
γέρων, old man

γῆ, earth, land
γίγνομαι, I become
γλῶττα, tongue
γράφω, I write
γυνή, woman, wife

δείκνυμι, I show
δεινός, terrible
δέκα, ten
δέκατος, tenth
δένδρον, tree
δεύτερος, second
δηλῶ, I show
Δημοσθένης, Demosthenes
διαφθείρω, I destroy, corrupt
δίδωμι, I give
δοῦλος, slave
δουλῶ, I enslave
δύναμις, power
δύο, two
δώδεκα, twelve
δωδέκατος, twelfth
δῶρον, gift, present.

ἔαρ, spring
ἕβδομος, seventh
ἐγώ, I
ἐθέλω, I am willing
εἰμί, I am
εἰς, into
εἷς, one
εἰσί(ν), they are
ἐκ, out of, from
ἐκεῖνος, that
ἕκτος, sixth
ἐκφεύγω, I escape
ἐλεύθερος, free
'Ελλάς, Greece
"Ελλην, Greek

ἐλπίς, hope
ἐμός, my
ἐν, in
ἕν, one (neuter of εἷς)
ἔνατος, ninth
ἕνδεκα, eleven
ἑνδέκατος, eleventh
ἐννέα, nine
ἕξ, six
ἐπιστολή, letter
ἐπιτίθεμαι, I attack
ἑπτά, seven
ἔργον, deed, labour, task, work
ἔρχομαι, I come, go
ἕστηκα, I stand
ἔστην, I stood
ἐστί(ν), is
ἔτος, year
εὖ, well
εὐγενής, noble
εὐρύς, broad, wide
εὔφρων, kind, kindly
ἔχω, I have, possess.

ζητῶ, I seek
ζυγόν, yoke.

ἡγεμών, leader
ἡδύς, sweet, pleasant, pleasing
ἡμέρα, day
ἡμέτερος, our.

θάλαττα, sea
θαυμάζω, I admire, wonder at
θεά, goddess
θεός, god
θέρος, summer
θηρεύω, I hunt, pursue
θύω, I sacrifice.

ἱερεύς, priest
ἱππεύς, horseman; plur. ἱππῆς,
  cavalry

ἵππος, horse
ἵστημι, I set up
ἰχθύς, fish.

καί, and
καί . . . καί, both . . . and
κακός, bad
κακῶς, badly
κακῶς ποιῶ, I treat badly, ill
κακῶς πράττω, I fare badly, ill
καλός, beautiful, honourable
καταλείπω, I leave behind
κελεύω, I order
κεφαλή, head
κῆρυξ, herald
κριτής, judge
κρούω, I strike
κωλύω, I prevent.

λαμβάνω, I take, receive
λέγω, I say, speak, tell
λείπω, I leave, forsake
λέων, lion
λιμήν, harbour
λόγος, word, speech
λύω, I loose, free, loosen, set free:
  middle λύομαι, I ransom.

μάχη, battle
μάχομαι, I fight
μέγας, big, great, large
μέλας, black
μένω, I remain, await, stay
μετά, with acc. after; with gen.
  with
μή, not
μήν, month
μήτηρ, mother
μία, one (fem. of εἷς)
μοῦσα, Muse.

ναῦς, ship

ναύτης, sailor
νεανίας, young man
νεώς, temple
νῆσος, island
νίκη, victory
νικῶ, I conquer, defeat ; οἱ νικῶντες, the conquerors ; οἱ νενικημένοι, the conquered
νόμος, law
νῦν, now
νύξ, night.

ὁ, ἡ, το, the
ὄγδοος, eighth
ὁδός, road
ὀδούς, tooth
οἰκία, house
ὀκτώ, eight
ὀξύς, sharp
ὅπλον, arm, weapon
ὄρος, mountain
ὁρῶ, I see
οὐ, not
οὗτος, this.

παιδεύω, I train
παῖς, boy, child, son
πάλαι, formerly
πᾶς, all, every, whole
πατήρ, father
πατρίς, native-country
παύω, I stop (transitive): middle
παύομαι, I cease
πέδαι, fetters
πείθω, I advise, persuade : middle
πείθομαι, I obey
πέμπτος, fifth
πέμπω, I send
πέντε, five
Πέρσης, Persian
πιστεύω, I believe, trust
πλούσιος, rich

ποιητής, poet
ποιῶ, I do, make ; εὖ ποιῶ, I
benefit, serve, treat well ; οἱ εὖ
ποιοῦντες, benefactors : κακῶς
ποιῶ, I treat badly, ill
πολέμιος, enemy
πόλεμος, war : τὸν πόλεμον ποιοῦμαι, I carry on the war
πόλις, city, state
πολίτης, citizen, fellow-citizen
πολλάκις, often
πολύς, much, many ; πολύ (adv.),
much, far : οἱ πολλοί, the many
πορεύομαι, I march
ποταμός, river
πρᾶγμα, affair
πράττω (trans.), I accomplish,
act, administer, manage, transact : (intrans.) fare
πρό, before, in front of
προδίδωμι, I betray
πρός, to (after τὸν πόλεμον ποιοῦμαι), against
προσβάλλω, I attack
πρῶτος, first
πύλη, gate.

ῥάδιος, easy
ῥαδίως, easily
ῥήτωρ, orator, rhetorician.

σείω, I shake, brandish
σός, thy, your (= Lat. tuus)
σοφία, wisdom
σοφός, wise, clever
σοφῶς, wisely
στέλλω, I equip, fit out
στρατηγός, general
στρατιά, army
στρατιώτης, soldier
στρατόπεδον, camp
σύ, thou
συγγράφω, I write a history

σῴζω, I save, keep, preserve
Σωκράτης, Socrates
σῶμα, body
σωφρόνως, temperately
σώφρων, temperate.

τάξις, rank
ταμίας, steward
τάττω, I draw up
ταχέως, quickly
τεῖχος, wall
τέταρτος, fourth
τέτταρες, four
τίθημι, I place, put, enact
τιμή, honour
τιμῶ, I honour
τότε, then
τρεῖς, three
τροπαῖον, trophy

ὑμέτερος, your (= Lat. *vester*)

ὑπέρ, for, on behalf of
ὑπό, by.

φεύγω, I fly, flee, flee from
φίλιος, friendly
φιλῶ, I love
φύλαξ, guard
φυλάττω, I guard.

χαλεπός, difficult, hard, troublesome
χαρίεις, graceful
χειμάν, winter
χρήσιμος, useful
χώρα, country.

ψεύδω, I deceive : (*middle* : ψεύδομαι, I lie, tell lies).

ὤ, O.

THE END